It is no Secret

DONNA MEEHAN

RANDOM HOUSE AUSTRALIA

Random House Australia Pty Ltd
20 Alfred Street, Milsons Point, NSW 2061
http://www.randomhouse.com.au

Sydney New York Toronto
London Auckland Johannesburg

First published 2000 by Random House Australia

National Library of Australia
Cataloguing-in-Publication Data

Meehan, Donna.
It is no secret.

ISBN 0 091 83994 7.

1. Meehan, Donna. 2. Meehan, Donna – Childhood and youth.
3. Aborigines, Australian – Biography. 4. Aborigines,
Australia – Women – Biography. I. Title.

305.89915

Typeset in 11.5/14 pt Bembo by Midland Typesetters
Printed and bound in Australia by Griffin Press

Designed by Greendot Design

10 9 8 7 6 5 4 3 2 1

This book is dedicated
To my loving husband, Ron
For our wonderful sons, Darren, Tim and Mark
And our grandchildren, Kiyarna and Beau

Contents

From Pilliga

WHO IS HE?

There I stood, lost in time, motionless, gazing into his love-filled dark brown eyes. Those beckoning eyes that had broken many, many hearts. Hundreds of women had yearned for him, both openly and secretly.

He was so handsome that his looks alone were sufficient to melt the heart strings of any woman. His soft, silky, deep voice sent shivers down their spines, and when he sang he had the power to take their breath away and woo women to the edge of fantasy.

Here I was, face to face, sinking into his deep enchanting eyes, falling in love with him also. I took slow, deep breaths. I had never seen such a masculine man before. My eyes became misty from the tide of emotions whirling inside me.

His skin was as sensual and smooth as velvet. I could all but touch him. I was close enough, but I couldn't. There was a barrier between us. After a few more seconds of being totally captive to him and oblivious to the other people in the room, who were all focused on me, and my reaction to this elegant male, I timidly stretched forth my fingers to feel him. Just for a second. Just one touch would satisfy me.

The cold, flat surface triggered me back to reality. It was only a photograph that had entranced me. I was too late. He had died a few decades ago, although one consolation was that he knew me. He was there the day I was born, anxiously awaiting those first sounds a newborn babe makes announcing its safe arrival into the world. He must have known I was going to be a dreamer. His loving arms cradled and nursed me and when I cried he would gently stroke my face and softly sing me back to sleep with the lyrics of one of his favourite songs, 'Beautiful Dreamer'.

His velvet lips kissed me and sealed me with his pride and love that would stay with me my entire life. He longed for the day I would return to his arms, but he could wait no longer. His lifetime had run out.

My fingers sadly traced around his profile in the large photograph that hung portentously on the lounge room wall in front of me. I stood, convincing myself that this was my father. With my heart pounding, I eventually asked the question while anticipating the answer. 'Who is he?' I nervously asked, directing my question to the adults in the room. The entire time I was in full view of my mother who sat at the kitchen table in the adjoining room. Proudly, she replied, 'That's your grandfather.'

THE STRONGEST ECHO OF MY PAST

T he strongest echo of my past is the sound of laughter. The memories of my early childhood are of being encircled by the laughter of my cousins, as we played freely in the warmth of the sun-glazed days. We either fell asleep at night to the rowdy encore of singing from my grandparents, aunties and mother, accompanied by the uncles on their guitars, or to the sound of drifting voices from the adults sharing stories and their insistent laughter. I don't think I ever knew what silence was, for when the voices died down, there was always the repetitive crackling of the fire, over which the billy hung.

Such carefree days. Life was simple. Days rolled into one another. Sunrise, sunset.

Grandfather, Jimmy Welsh, was working for a white property owner as a helping hand and labourer, and he managed to get permission to set up camp for his family at one end of the property. Our camp was on the Walgett end of town, now known as Broad Street. The camp consisted of a few huts erected out of corrugated iron or 'tin iron', as my uncles called it, usually retrieved from the dump. They were small, one-room buildings which served their purpose, simply to provide shelter for sleep or from rain. It was a happy camp with the family looking after each other and sharing everything from food to treasures found at the dump. No-one was greedy or wanting something from someone else as everyone had their turn to enjoy the find.

There was always plenty of advice on hand between the knowledge and life experiences of the grandparents and adults. The older children automatically took on their roles to protect the younger children and keep them amused. It was the role of the men to bring home game and the role of the women to cook. Even the cooking was shared and we ate everything on our plates as we were too poor to be fussy. When there was no game, we lived on johnny cakes cooked on the open fire. Johnny cakes served as birthday cakes and Christmas cakes. They were the only standby for unexpected visitors and were usually cooked before the billy boiled.

The only concern for me was which cousin I would play with the next day or which game we would play first. There wasn't a worry in the world. Not for us kids at least, as our world only extended as far as our camp with our mother, brothers, sisters, aunts, uncles, cousins and the grandparents. Most of our time was occupied by climbing a favourite tree. This was a twelve-foot gum tree that stood only fifty feet away from our huts.

One day my eldest brother Barry came home from the corner shop bursting with some important news. This was when he was about eight years old. He told us kids to stop playin and to gather around him. He proudly announced the circus was coming to town.

Being only four, I had no understanding of what that meant but as he explained what type of animals would be there and the circus life, his enthusiasm was so infectious that all us kids became as excited as him.

We all jumped up and down and clapped our hands with delight, talking all at once and causing such a commotion that our mother hurried over to find out what was going on. We tried to explain the circus story all at once but Mum couldn't hear from all the noise and squeals. She stood amazed at the seven dark little pleading faces all wrapped in smiles from one end to the other, the brown eyes that shined like stars, begging her to let them go to the circus to see the animals. Four of the children were her own and the others were her nephews and niece. I am sure it must have hurt her much more than it hurt us when she had to say, 'It costs money to go there and we don't have any.'

That night all the little children at the camp lay in bed dejected. Only their frequent sighs interrupted the stillness in the bedroom. No-one felt like sleeping. We were so used to going off to sleep with untroubled minds, but tonight we were too sad. We had only been in bed for a short while, although it felt like forever, when we heard the three uncles returning home from work up camp. Uncle Barney, Uncle Cliffy and Uncle Billy used to set rabbit traps and sell furs. Sometimes they had local work and other times they could be gone for a week or two. Sometimes even longer.

Barry jumped out of bed to make the most of the opportune timing. We overheard him telling the uncles, in an important tone of voice, how the circus was in town and how the little ones would love to go and see the animals. We strained our ears to hear their reply but no-one spoke. We could hear a faint strum from a guitar and then the next sound we heard was Grandfather playing the button accordion and singing, 'He's Got the Whole World in His Hands'.

I lay back down in bed thinking we were not allowed to go. Just when I was snuggled down under the dark grey army blanket, Barry returned and came over to our bunks and placed two bob each in our hands. We gasped and snuggled down tightly squeezing the coins between our hands or placing them under our pillows. We had just been given the world and were much too excited to sleep, impatient for the sunrise, but after a lot of whispering and giggling, we eventually fell asleep with smiles on our faces.

THE CIRCUS

The next day the call of the currawongs awakened us as usual but it was a very, very special day for us kids. The circus didn't start until three o'clock and it seemed like we couldn't find anything to keep us busy or keep us from thinking about the fun at the circus. It seemed we were waiting for eternity to pass. The camp looked the same. The adults were yarning the same but to us it felt different. We didn't even want to listen to the adults' conversations. The air was filled with excitement. It felt like we had a new toy but there was no toy. Nothing interested us unless it was about big tops and animals. It seemed forever, waiting for lunchtime. Then Mum told us it was time to get cleaned up. At last, we could make tracks to the circus.

We had to walk into town, about three miles away. After Barry had promised Mum he would take care of us all, we set off on our big adventure. Barry led the way, naturally, as he was the eldest. Then there was Widdy the second eldest, myself, and Bronco and Maxi, our cousins. As we walked towards town we met up with other kids, some black, some white, who were also going to see the great circus.

When we arrived at the circus camp we couldn't believe our eyes. The red, white and orange tent was the biggest thing we had ever seen. We checked out all the animals in the cages and noticed their strange smell. It was the first time we had ever seen lions, elephants, monkeys and tigers. It was a magical adventure. There was loud music coming from big speakers, the smell of food everywhere. There were clowns with funny coloured hair, wearing funny clothes. One of them was wearing the wrong shoes and kept falling over himself. All the people were happy and talking about the clowns and animals. There were lots of people from town walking around all dressed up. This was an important day for them too.

Barry talked us into spending our money on food, lollies and ice-cream. He told us we could get inside the big tent for nothing. We never questioned his ideas; we believed he knew everything and trusted him instinctively. Just as we were finishing our ice-creams, the circus manager was telling everyone over the speakers to round up and take their seats.

We joined the slow-moving queue along with the adults and white children, when Barry beckoned us to follow him, saying he knew a short cut. We followed him around the great tent, weaving in and out of the long poles that helped the tent to stand up, until we were at what seemed to be the back of the tent. Barry lifted the heavy flap and told us to squeeze between the flap and the grass and wriggle through like a snake until we made it to the other side. When the last child made it through safely, we marched confidently behind Barry straight to the front row, took our seats innocently and waited for the show to begin.

I marvelled at the giant swing that hung from the roof and wished I could swing on it when I grew up. I nearly lost my breath as I watched the lady on the swing. I loved her costume that was sky blue with silver stars stuck all over the front. All the children clapped and cheered. The boys whistled. Some of the little kids were scared stiff by the wild animals but when the clowns came out they laughed again at their jokes and tricks. We laughed so much that day, it was such good fun.

We always had to be home before dark, so when the sun started to set we slowly walked home. We all took turns saying what we wanted to be in the circus when we grew up. Uncle Cliffy met us along the way, probably just making sure we were coming back to camp. Then we all repeated the conversation, telling him what we wanted to be. I said I wanted to be the lady on the trapeze. Bronco wanted to be a clown. Widdy wanted to care for the animals and Barry wanted to be the Ringmaster, of course. It was all too exciting. I wanted to be grown up right there and then. Uncle listened patiently with a huge smile on his face and when we finished he told us that when our grandfather was younger, he used to work in a circus and perform acrobatics across the tops of horses. We felt real proud knowing that our grandfather did that. Barry couldn't wait to get to school to tell the other children. I wished I was at school to tell someone but I was too young, so I decided to tell my tree.

I suppose I could be forgiven for thinking the next day that it had all been a beautiful dream, but no, it did happen and the circus was our favourite topic for weeks to follow. We asked Grandfather every night to tell us about when he worked at the circus. Not only did he do tricks on the horses, but he got paid to sing to the audience. He was called 'The Singing Welshman from Pilliga'.

THE WHITE SANTA MAN

The weather was getting hotter. We had glorious orangey-red sunsets and we spent our free time swimming and fishing in the river. Barry began to talk about a white Santa man. He told all the kids at the camp about this white fella who wore a red suit and brought lollies, toys and food, all free. We didn't know, but he knew that Christmas Day was coming soon.

All the men made sure they finished the shearing and trapping to make it home to Grandfather's camp for Christmas, and all of my aunties and cousins came to camp for the holidays, so there were many people and lots of cousins to play with. We had lots of singalongs, shared stories about the funny things the kids said and did, or heard stories from my uncles about shearing and trapping. There were always yarns about other men on the road looking for paid work. Then there were all the funny stories. My favourite was about how an emu chased Uncle Billy all over a paddock when he tried to pinch its eggs. Uncle Billy was such a good storyteller that although we heard that story a hundred times, us kids laughed as much as we did the very first time he told us.

The adults loved eating emu eggs and my grandfather could carve beautiful pictures on the eggshells. It would take many days to carve a picture and each one was different. Us kids used to sit for hours just watching him, how he used to scratch the shell with a sharp knife. There were seven layers on the egg and the different layers gave varied colours from black, grey, bluey-grey and cream depending how deep he carved in. Carving was so dangerous we all thought he would cut off his fingers. While Grandfather carved away Uncle Barney kept him company under the gum tree. They would sit in silence for a long, long time, or at times Uncle Barney would play a gum leaf; at other times we would hear the drifting sound of him playing his mouth organ. Some of the tunes were songs in the lingo the old people spoke, some were from church, but my favourite was always 'Beautiful Dreamer'.

On Christmas morning after our breakfast of toast from the fire, we played in the dirt eagerly waiting for the white Santa man. We scratched our names with a twig into the soft red dirt. We drew pictures of dolls, bikes and animals. We spelled out words trying to fill in time. My cousins Doll-Doll and Teresa played with pieces of broken brown bottle glass, pretending it was furniture for their imaginary doll house. The boys rolled a broken bucket around the paddock while the adults sat in the shade of the tree catching up on the news about people from Pilliga where Grandfather used to live. We got so much education listening to

yarns about life on missions in Walgett, Bourke and Brewarrina. Sometimes we would hear the women cry but
didn't know why and we weren't told when we asked.
Aunty Agnes, Aunty Joan and Aunty Audrey were what we
called the cry-babies because when they drank they would
always end up crying and being sad.

It was still quite early in the morning and as we played
in the dirt we constantly watched the track that led from
the flat to the camp for any sign of the white Santa man.
Uncle Allan spotted some dust whirling from the distance.
He told us kids to keep watching the rising dust. Then Barry
jumped up and yelled, "'E's 'ere, 'ere 'e comes. 'E's comin,
yep, it's 'im.' A minute later, sure enough, all of us, adults
and children alike, could see the light blue Holden utility.
Every eye was on the ute. Squeals of delight came from the
kids who were filled with hopeful hearts.

The ute finally came to a stop. All the children surrounded the vehicle and slowly and shyly the adults came
closer. Santa stepped out of the cabin and climbed up into
the back of the ute. The children pushed forward expec-
tantly, our faces lit with dazzling white smiles which could
only be compared to the white of Santa's beard. He started
to hand out toys and sweets to us kids. Then there were
cakes and lipsticks for the women and cigarettes for the
men. I received a small doll and a book, and although they
were second-hand, to us they were brand new as we knew
no better. Each child was given a small bag of lollies and
we had good fun swapping and bargaining for each other's
favourite lolly.

We didn't have an imitation Christmas tree or ornaments
as such, but after we unwrapped the gifts, the kids tore the
paper into strips and tied them on the gum tree. It was

funny watching the currawongs hopping from branch to branch being inquisitive about their swaying companions. It took about a week for them to remove all the pretty paper and reclaim their ownership.

As soon as we had opened our gifts, Barry had planned our next escapade. Arms around the older kids, he whispered his plan. We all threw our toys inside the tin shack and took off like a gust of wind. Mum yelled, 'Where you kids goin?' Barry faced her and, running backwards, answered, 'We're goin to see what the Fernando kids got.' The Fernandos lived in the next camp downstream, about half a mile away. It was a matter of running barefoot, fast as horses, crossing a river bed and bank which probably wasn't too steep but, to a four-year-old, may as well have been a mountain. Our feet were so tough and the rough track never worried us, but we had to keep a sharp eye out for broken glass and run between thorns and spurs. We knew not to handle cutting grass which would slice your hand open, and as we ran through the trees and the overgrowth we knew to keep an eye out for snakes. We made excellent time.

We had only been at the Fernandos' camp long enough to stop panting before we heard the revving of an engine. A moment later all the kids in the camp were shouting, 'Santa, Santa's 'ere, Santa's 'ere.' Once again the kids and adults besieged the ute and gratefully accepted the presents. There were about twenty people in this camp. I was standing right beside the driver's door opening my present when Santa leaned forward to the driver and said, 'Bob, all these kids look the same to me!' I giggled and giggled behind the back of my hand.

We laughed all the way home. Barry was so clever to

outsmart Santa. We never once felt guilty about doubling up. I think the adults found it more amusing than us when we explained the real reason for bolting off. Aunty Tam kept shaking her head and saying, 'That poor man. Barry, you got no shame.' Then a great roar of laughter went up from all the men and all the women. The adults had tears rolling down their cheeks. They were happy times, and we always found something to have a good laugh about.

That was Christmas Day, no stress, no trimmings, no fancy cooking. The kids content with their second-hand toys, the women with their lipsticks and cakes, all the men sitting under the tree smoking tobacco, and the choir of currawongs above them.

Singing Around the Campfire

The uncles' visits at camp were special times for both the women and for us kids too. They were the roving newspaper, keeping the camp informed about what was happening to Aboriginal people all over the state. We tried to sneak up on the adults to overhear their conversations but we were always sent off to play. Even Barry couldn't outsmart the uncles.

The boys used to make shanghais (slingshots) and bull-roarers for amusement, but most of their time was spent playing some form of sport, football, boxing, running or kicking a ball around. Occasionally the men would bring home marbles which had to be shared amongst the boys. The girls occupied themselves with imaginary dolls and dolls furniture from pieces of broken bottle glass. We played hide-and-seek, climbed trees, or built bark cubbies to pass the time. We played with balls and bike wheels found at the dump and if we got bored we could always chase the dogs or go for a walk in the dry river bed.

We were returning from the river bed one hot sunny day when we heard lovely music coming from our camp, a different sound to what we were accustomed to. Not the button accordion, guitar or even the violin that were so familiar. We couldn't even pick who was singing. We could see the camp people sitting under the tree and we raced each other to see who could get back home first. When we all made it to the tree, strangely enough the adults were all seated around a peculiar square box. They told us it was a wind-up gramophone and no matter how many times we asked how and what made it work, we couldn't understand. It was a new toy for the adults but the kids weren't allowed to touch it.

Grandfather had traded something for it after he sang for the local shearers on a property, and felt so proud bringing it home to share with the camp. Grandfather, who was well known for his lovely tenor voice, was also a great musician. He knew how to make a violin talk. He also played the piano accordion, button accordion, gum leaf and the spoons. When Grandfather lived at Pilliga he was known as the Singing Welshman. He was asked to all the birthday parties so our family really filled in as the band. All of his daughters inherited the singing voice. He was thrilled about the gramophone as he had been wanting one for many years but had no money to purchase one.

Obtaining records was difficult in those times. Most of them came from the treasures found at the dump but occasionally someone would earn a near-new one which would be highly treasured. These were played continuously until they were worn away. Our family was musically gifted and perhaps in one way the gramophone enhanced the grown-ups' appreciation for music, however it also captivated and influenced them. Consequently they began to sing the new songs more and more. We were transitional people, not traditional. When country and western music arrived at the camp from about 1940 onwards it was heartily embraced by all. Even the language of the new music was different – it had a new twang. We were told it was all the way from a camp called America, a long way walkabout.

STEALING APPLES

Our grandmother was Madeline White. She lived at Quambone. Grandfather met her when he had a couple of months' work there. Work was scarce but the men travelled around taking any type of work offered to them. After they married, our grandparents moved around between the Pilliga, Gulargambone and Coonamble districts, wherever they could pick up a couple of bob for work.

The Aboriginal camp on the east side of Coonamble was referred to as Tin Town as all the shacks were erected out of tin. My grandparents, Mum and her brothers and sisters spent many happy days here, after they moved from Pilliga in the mid-1940s. Although living conditions were rough and we were neither wanted nor respected by the white people, such camps were a great support, socially, psychologically and spiritually. The women shared food and clothing and looked out for one another's kids. The men had plenty of business to discuss, sharing with one another any hint of rumours where work was available. We were the dispossessed. Herded onto the outskirts of town. Out of sight and out of mind. We weren't given any community nurses or counsellors in those days, as white people had no idea or understanding of the blacks' fight for survival. So the camps served a vital function for support, and were the true meaning of community.

Grandmother gave birth to eleven children: Clifford, Beatrice, Thelma, Bertrum, Hilton, Ivy, Dot, Doris, Agnes, Joan, and Audrey. The utility from the Aboriginal Inland Mission would drop off boxes filled with clothes, shoes and blankets at Tin Town. We were told they came from rich white people in the city. The clothes served their purpose as big families like Grandmother's were common in those days and no-one had the money to buy such things. Even the men and women enjoyed trying on their new clothes. The first couple of days after the drop-off were like a big fashion parade. It was living theatre watching the adults strutting around like proud peacocks in their new clothes and hats.

Women always wore dresses in those days. One time we nearly wet ourselves laughing as we listened to Aunty Joan complaining about some sort of netting petticoat now attached to the latest fashions, which was scratching her leg. She couldn't understand the reason why white women had it on their clothes. She thought for a long time it was to wear fishing and then she wondered if it was to keep the mosquitoes out. The netting made no sense to any of the young Aboriginal women and they couldn't understand why the white women thought it was necessary. In frustration and desperation she tore off the netting and went for a walk into town. Aunty was gone for several hours and by the time she returned she was as cranky as a mule. Due to the constant friction of walking, she now had one continuous rash around her waist where the edging had been scratching her all day. It was so painful and made her that wild, that this was probably the reason she was turned off wearing dresses forever.

The men teased her about the incident for weeks, reminding her how angry she was when she stormed home that afternoon swearing her head off about the stupid idiotic dress and telling everyone she would rather go back to wearing laplaps. We had no need for TV as we always had something to laugh about. It was comforting for us kids to fall asleep in the camp listening to all the different families laughing. Laughing was healing, an important and necessary part of our survival.

Grandfather often told stories about growing up in the bush with his family and how they ate bush tucker. Camping was a way of life. Grandfather shared many campfires with white swaggies who had a lot in common with him, seeking any kind of work to help support his family. Grandfather and Uncle Bert were builders. They carted wood from the sawmill at Pilliga to Walgett and Wilcannia. Grandfather and Uncle Bert built most of the houses for the first mission at Walgett and were part of the team which built the mission at Wilcannia. In between building contracts, Grandfather would fall back on sheep shearing, at which he was highly skilled.

When the men found work on stations, they slept out under the stars around a campfire as it was unheard of them sleeping in the labourers' huts with the permanent white hands. Equality had not yet been conceived, it was more than a dream away.

The men in our camp would kill kangaroos and emus or bring a sheep. Whenever we didn't have these, more than likely we had a feed of fish. If the men were all away and it was bad weather, we lived off johnny cakes, and even at times just bread and water. Hunger can lead people to take extra risks and so, through sheer desperation, we would sometimes scramble through the fence at a nearby orchard and steal apples and oranges.

One day we got caught in the act. Barry had convinced us kids that seeing we were so hungry and there was an orchard full of fruit, if it wasn't picked it would just fall off the trees anyway and rot. It was better for us to eat it than let it go to waste so we agreed we would help the farmer out.

All four of us had our arms full of fresh sweet-smelling fruit when the farmer suddenly appeared, frightening the daylights out of us. Three of us ran off leaving Barry to deal with the irate farmer. When safe in the distance we stopped and listened to the farmer chastising our poor brother, but we were too fearful to go back and take our share of the blame. The farmer, a tall man with huge muscles, over-towered my brother. He had grabbed Barry's collar and was yelling at him, ending up the encounter by giving him a bit of a kick up the backside before sending him on his way.

We were so relieved when our brother rejoined us. But like water off a duck's back, Barry laughed it all off as if nothing much had happened, saying, 'There's nothin to worry about. I told him us kids had no food at the camp and he said, "You can have it this once but don't do it again."'

We all patted Barry, thinking he was very brave and afraid of nothing. Then we dismissed it and simply enjoyed the delicious fruit. Later that night as we sat around the campfire Barry admitted that he had been stealing apples almost all his life. I suspect the old farmer had seen him many times. He must have chuckled to himself imagining that Barry thought he was real smart taking fruit without being caught. Maybe he believed that the stern talk frightened us kids away for good. How his heart was saddened when he learned the truth about why the little dark kids never returned.

Joy Ride

Joy Ride

The first train ride I took is as clear in my mind as if it had happened yesterday.

Mum had all us kids dressed up, our hair brushed, which was only done for special days, and we were constantly reminded to use our manners. Barry, Widdy, Robby, Sooty and myself were put in the back seat of a taxi while Mum sat in the front with the taxi driver. The lady taxi driver had known all the kids at the camp since their birth and I thought it was strange that she and Mum didn't speak as we made our way along the bumpy red track leading from camp towards town.

As I watched the red dust swirling from behind the vehicle, I remembered we were all dressed up and on our way to the station for my first ride on the big steam train. We had always heard the faint train whistle from camp, and a few times we saw the clouds of smoke from the train, but

I had never seen one close up. I sat impatiently in the back seat clicking my shiny new black shoes together and admiring the new dress I'd been given for the day. All my brothers also wore their new shoes with white socks, a white shirt and a little black bow tie. We knew everyone had to get dressed up to go on the train and we felt important, like the little rich kids from town who often had train rides during the holidays.

When we arrived at the station we were surprised to see so many other kids and women waiting on the platform. All the children were happy and running in between the legs of their mothers, playing tips to fill in time. It wouldn't be long before the huge powerful black train pulled into the station as we could see its dirty grey smoke pouring into the air half a mile away. It was a rare treat for us kids at camp to climb into one of the uncles' old cars and be driven into town, so, when Mum said it was time to take our seat on the train, we climbed aboard jubilantly, anticipating the joy ride.

We took a few minutes to decide who would have the window seat or sit near the aisle, then we kept changing places to decide who'd sit next to whom. Mum hadn't taken her seat yet, so we all took turns inspecting the toilet which fascinated us. We knew it wouldn't be long before the train pulled out so we took our seats again, but then we realised we'd lost Sooty and Robby. When an old white woman in a red hat sat next to me, I changed seats with Barry, as she terrified me. Suddenly I felt scared. 'Where's Mum?' I asked Barry, who kept telling us, 'Mum'll be gettin on the train in a minute.' I kept asking him where were Sooty, Robby and Mum and he said, 'They must be in the next car.' There were still lots of black women standing on the platform hugging one another.

With a sudden jerk, squealing of brakes and a loud puff of the steam engine, the train shunted forward. Fear gripped my heart. Barry and Widdy had bewildered looks on their faces, glancing at me and then at each other. I stared out of the window as we slowly pulled out of the station. I was very confused by all the women standing on the platform watching us and wailing. Then I saw her. There was my mum in her only good blue dress standing next to my aunts and our old grandmother. Just standing there. Standing there with tears rolling down their cheeks too fast to wipe away. Then Mum waved a white hanky and I pressed my face against the window pane as hard as I could, watching her. Watching until her blue dress faded into a tiny dot of colour. I looked back at the station for as long as I could until it was out of sight.

The atmosphere of celebration and anticipation that had filled the cabin vanished, and there now echoed the distressed calls of frightened, broken-hearted children. 'Why didn't Mum and Grandma get on the train?' I cried over and over. The white woman in the red hat sat beside me with clasped hands, expressionless. Barry reassured me: 'Mum'll catch the next train. I'll look after you.' But he was crying too. I didn't understand what had happened, why Mum had changed her mind or why she would let us go anywhere without our aunty or grandmother to look after us.

We were on that train for a very long time. As the hours ticked by, I ran out of tears to cry. I sat with my back to the white woman and my face near the window so I could feel the breeze on my face. The flat country from home covered with warm red dirt was now very hilly and layered with trees, and the camps alongside the train track became

larger and more frequent. The white woman corrected
Barry as she overheard him telling Widdy and me that they
were the camps of the white man, saying, 'They are called
towns and we are going to the city.'

The motion of the noisy train became monotonous and
the heat of the day invaded the cabin. It was a long time
between the bigger towns now. We saw flash houses and
colourful gardens but very few people on the streets. I
couldn't see any dumps or orchards. Barry was telling
Widdy that all the blackfellas must be away working, as
there weren't any to be seen in the towns or bush we passed.
All we saw were white people. Now and then we heard
youngens on the train sobbing. After a while, bored by the
countryside, I fell asleep despite the sting in my eyes from
having cried so much that morning.

When I woke, we were still on the train. It was dark and
I was cold. Barry and Widdy huddled together against the
cold; the white woman gave me a tea towel to keep warm
as there was no blanket. The noise of the train tracks, the
rattle of bridges, the crying children and biting mozzies got
annoying. I sat there reliving the events of the day, always
coming up with more questions than when I began.

All three of us took turns sitting next to the white
woman. She still scared me with her silence and her
unfriendly face, nothing at all like the people back at camp
or even the happy strangers we saw at the circus that day.
I was homesick. It had been the longest and most confusing
day of my life. I felt alone in the dark. The tears still stung
my eyes, hurting more than the mozzies as I realised for the
first time in my life there was no-one to sing me to sleep.
It must have been the longest night in my life.

When I awoke the next time it was daylight. Barry and

Widdy were still asleep. I wished they would wake up, as I had so many questions to ask. This wasn't the joy ride I thought was going to be so much fun. Suddenly I felt this awful pain inside, something I'd never felt before. I felt like screaming and waking my two brothers. I burst into tears and sobbed so hard that I did wake them. I sobbed and sobbed and lost my breath so I couldn't talk. After a few minutes I calmed down enough to mumble, 'Where we goin?' Barry didn't know. He suggested we wait at the next train station till Mum's train pulled in. We were so hungry by this time. The white woman pulled out some sandwiches from her large old brown bag and shared them with us. We seemed to chew in time with the clicketty clack of the train tracks. I was so bored looking at the same faces of the few people I could see in the train, as I was in the window seat and we weren't allowed to walk around except to go to the toilet. The walls and ceiling inside the train were a drab dark brown colour and the seats a lighter brown, so I concentrated on the bright red and yellow pattern on my new dress. Of course, it wasn't brand new, as Mum had gone into town the day before and returned with an armful of clothes for us kids. She said she got them from the Aboriginal Inland Mission.

I could hear some children fighting over their seats; I seemed to notice every cough and every sigh. It was very hot and I was glad we could have the window open a little so I could feel the fresh breeze on my face and sometimes even catch a scent of the bush from the trees we passed. At times I sat between my brothers but when it got too hot or uncomfortable I would go back to my seat next to the white woman. She never spoke. Occasionally, she would pull a mirror from her brown bag and comb her hair or put on lipstick. She would read for a little while from a newspaper, then fold it up and put it back in her bag. I wondered what else she had inside that bag.

Finally, Widdy and Barry were told they had to get off at the next station but I wasn't allowed to go with them. Barry was upset and told the white woman, 'Mum said I 'ave to look after the other kids. I promised,' but she ushered the boys out of the train saying, 'I'll look after Donna. You'll see your brothers and sister very soon.' Sad, frightened and alone, I looked at my brothers as our train pulled out of the station. I didn't notice who was with them or how many people were on the platform, it seemed to happen so fast. It was just awful. It made no sense. My heart was so frightened and confused, but what could a five-year-old do about it?

The white woman sat with me and talked every now and then, but I kept looking out the window. After some time she pointed outside. I looked, and there was the biggest dam I ever saw. The woman explained that I was looking at boats, as I didn't know what they were, not having seen them before. They looked pretty sitting there on top of the water. The sun skipped across the surface, making it look like someone was throwing hundreds of stars into the water. It made me happy seeing the stars dancing on top of the water. It was so beautiful that I wished I could just sit there and watch the water and the boats for a long time, but I was stuck on the horrible train. I was told this was the Hawkesbury River and that we didn't have far to go now as we were getting off at Newcastle. Then the beautiful shiny water was out of sight.

My bottom was stiff from sitting for so long in a confined space. The train travelled very slowly now as we meandered through hills and then alongside the river. There were lots of trees and the smell of the bush was strong. I could hear birds singing up in the trees but I couldn't see them because they were hiding. The size of the green hills impressed me as the ground back home was flat and this was all new to me. I felt we were very high up on a hill now as I could see the tops of trees leading down to the river. I couldn't see any ground at all, just hundreds of trees. I wouldn't want to go for a walk in that bush as I knew there would be too many snakes; but I liked all the different shades of green from all the different trees. To help pass the time, I took particular notice of the leaves. Some of them had yellow tips and others red. Small purple flowers grew on a vine that climbed freely around tree trunks and even acted as an umbrella for smaller trees. The bush smelled crisp and fresh, different to the old bush from home. Now and then I could hear birds calling, and when I heard the frightened call of a young bird I could identify with it. For the first time, I too felt like a trapped, helpless baby bird.

I was interrupted by the white woman who went to the toilet and returned with a wet tea towel with which she briskly washed my face. She brushed my hair, then combed her hair with another brush and applied red lipstick and re-placed her gloves and her red hat.

As I looked out of the window, I could see a big town coming into view with lots of big houses and cars. She told me that this was a town called Newcastle. There was a screeching of brakes and a hissing of the steam engine. In between the clouds of steam and coal smoke, I could see lots of people standing on the platform. Only one thing was wrong, but it took a minute for me to work it out: all the people here were white. There were no other dark-skinned people, or blackfellas as my uncle called them.

After a lot of shunting, the train eventually came to a halt. The woman told me it was time to get off. She took my hand and I followed. There were so many people. I was trying to see where Robby and Sooty were, but I was too short and I couldn't see anything except white legs and lots of suitcases. There was a lot of noise from people talking and laughing. There were men in black uniforms getting suitcases off the train and other men loading boxes onto it. Another man had a whistle that he liked blowing. There was another man yelling, telling people where they could catch the next train. Everyone was busy.

By this time there was another boy with me but I didn't know who he was. He looked like he was a couple of years older than me. We were much too frightened to speak, so we just sat on a bench where we'd been told to sit and wait. The woman in the red hat went to get us a drink. I stared around looking for a familiar face but I was lost in the crowd. All the men and women were wearing hats and gloves like the people at the circus. All the women wore lipstick, and I knew they got that from the white Santa man.

Just when I felt like getting up and running away, the woman returned along with a tall dark man and a short white woman. The two strangers bent over towards me, smiling and saying, 'Hello, Donna.' The woman told me: 'This is your new mummy and daddy. They have a lovely house and animals. Now you go with them and they'll give you something to eat.'

They took my hand and led me away through the station and down a paved street where lots of different coloured cars were parked in a row. I even saw a ute, but it wasn't the white Santa man's car, it was a green one. I kept looking around for my brothers, or at least one of them, as I didn't want to go anywhere without them. They told me to sit in the back seat of a creamy-coloured car that was the same shape as the white Santa man's car. Then I saw another car following us and I told myself Barry and the other boys were in that one and we were all going to the same camp.

A NEW CAMP CALLED HOME

I sat in the back seat of the car not speaking. The new dark man and white woman spoke in another language and even though I didn't understand a word, I could see they were very happy. The woman regularly turned around and looked at me with a bright smile. I didn't smile back, just lowered my head and kept my eyes fixed on the floor of the car. I was still very frightened, but I could see that these people were more friendly than the woman on the train. These were friendly strangers.

The car trip only took a little while. When we stopped, I could see the new camp which had a big white wooden house, lots of chickens and even a sheep or two. The house stood at the end of a dirt track and was surrounded by bush. I could smell the bush, so friendly and inviting. I could hear lots of happy birds whistling and talking to one another, and the chickens made me laugh as I watched them fighting with each other.

I heard a train in the distance, and the closer it got to the house the more nervous I became. I suppose I thought I would be put on it for another long trip. I was pleased to see it pass straight by the house, and was just starting to feel safe again when I heard another vehicle arriving. It turned into the yard where we stood watching the train, and two older people got out. I thought this must be the aunt and uncle of the people who lived at this camp.

I waited for my brothers to climb out of the car but the old people were by themselves. I was very disappointed. The two older people made a big fuss over me, talking to me, but I wasn't talking to anybody that day. They told me how pretty I was and how pretty my new dress was. They took photos of me standing between the man and woman in whose car I travelled. We stood in front of the chicken shed for a photo.

This was the day I arrived in Newcastle. It was 22 April 1960. I learned I had been collected from Broadmeadow Railway Station and then driven to my new home at Whitebridge, a suburb south of Newcastle. In time I learned the name of my new foster parents, Mr and Mrs Tim Popov. The older couple who welcomed me to Newcastle were their good friends Mr and Mrs Reedman, from Adamstown.

Everything was different. The people, the house, the food, no other kids around. My new mum and dad were very loving towards me. It took many weeks for me to get used to my new dad as he was a very tall, strong man and I was afraid of his size. I would hide behind the kitchen door every day when he returned from work. I wasn't very familiar with men as I had always been looked after by my mum or aunts around the camp. I only saw my uncles briefly, and women had a strong influence upon me. The men were left to influence the young boys.

Every day I remembered the camp, along with things like the circus, the white Santa man and the track that led to the river. I thought, Where are my brothers and all the people from the camp? What has happened to them all? But at the same time, I soon became familiar with the new white house that had rooms inside. I loved playing with the tap water as I had never seen water flowing out of a pipe before. I spent my days running around the little farm chasing chickens or sheep, as there wasn't a dog to play with.

The first gift Mr and Mrs Reedman gave me was something I highly valued. It was my very own little red table and chairs set. Someone from one of the churches gave me my first golliwog and another lady at another church gave me my first brand-new teddy bear. These became my constant companions. I named the golliwog Barry and the teddy bear Widdy, after my two eldest brothers. That way they were with me every day of my life. I talked to them and kissed them and this made me feel close to them, but how I wished they could come and live with me at this new camp called home.

FIRST FRIENDS

My new mum played a piano accordion just like my first mum. She would practise new songs through the week and every time I heard the accordion I would remember my first mum. The music was different but it still made me feel sad and lonely. The Popovs were also devout church-goers. Going to church was new but in time I got used to it. Mr Reedman was a lay preacher and regularly asked my new mum to sing. I used to sit up straight at church when she stood out the front and sang. While she was singing I would remember the camp, and everyone laughing and singing along. After church a lot of women used to gather around my mum and me and make a fuss over me.

Sundays became special days after I got used to church, and for years we spent our Sundays there. I loved it because this was when I met other children, at Sunday School. I loved the singing. Once I even sang my grandfather's special song, 'He's Got the Whole World in His Hands'. I especially liked the stories and the pretty pictures in the story books. After church we often went to a big park that was filled with the prettiest flowers that danced in the wind. It was just like in the picture books. Lots of people would go to this park after church, with their picnic lunch and in their Sunday clothes, and it was a lovely way to spend Sundays. The park was called King Edward Park, which was very close to the ocean.

From King Edward Park, I could see the ocean and the big boats that floated on top of it. I loved just sitting in the cool green grass and watching the beauty of the sun dancing on top of the water. My spirit would soar above the waves and as I was mesmerised by the intoxicating beauty of the ocean, here I virtually breathed freedom, daydreaming and wasting many hours simply enjoying this means of survival.

The squalling of seagulls would bring me back down to earth. The seagulls intrigued me because they had no fear and would come quite close to the people, knowing they would be fed scraps from the lunches. I laughed as I watched them fight over food or even rouse at another bird if it got too greedy. The smell of the salt air was a new scent to me and took a while to get accustomed to it. My little heart missed the smell of the red dirt, the tickle of the dry dust up my nostrils and the smell of the open campfire, but most of all I missed my tree and the cousins I played with every day. That's probably why I looked forward to Sunday School each week, just to be with other children my own age.

My first friends were children from the Lynch family at Whitebridge. Bronwyn was a teenager and was in the choir at church and she had a younger sister and a brother, but I can't remember their names. Once they gave me the most gorgeous dress I ever saw, much prettier than any I had ever seen in the picture books. It was made out of red material that had little bubbly dots, and red was my colour as it complemented my dark brown skin. The dress had a matching petticoat and was set off by a wide satin waistband which tied up at the back into a large bow. It was the type of dress every little girl wished for. I felt like a princess in it and couldn't wait until Sundays to wear it. It was nothing like any of the clothes we got back at the camp. I wished I could show it to my aunties, especially Aunty Tam, as she'd always thought I was special for some reason.

Late one afternoon there was a knock at the back door and there stood the Lynch kids. I didn't know it was my birthday until they handed me a present. It was a little doll that lay in a straw carry basket. Bronwyn had sewn a little blanket to cover the doll. I had turned six, and this was the first birthday I can ever remember celebrating.

That day was also memorable for another reason. The children couldn't stay long as a wild storm was brewing and they had to walk home through thick bush past the old Burwood Colliery at Whitebridge, which would take twenty minutes if they hurried. They would have just reached their house when the heavens opened up. I was amazed as I stood and watched lightning, and stones falling out of the sky. Dad told me it was called hail. I knew what dust storms were and had often seen willy-willys, but never hail. I ran around the yard collecting as many hailstones as I could, filling the carry basket with them and hoping to save them for always. From that day on whenever I saw hail it reminded me of my sixth birthday and sharing it with my first friends in the city, along with the wonder and joy of my first thunderstorm.

WHITEBRIDGE

Our house and property was at the end of a quarter mile dirt track that ran off Baroomba Street in Whitebridge. The train track ran alongside the front of the property. As I sat in my little red chair looking out the window, I often thought if I followed the track it would take me back home to the blackfellas' camp, but I also knew it was far, far away. I had such a fear of trains, due to that first terrifying experience, that one day Mum took me for a joy ride into Newcastle to meet Dad at work, to try and overcome my fear. We boarded the train at Whitebridge and got off at Hamilton railway station. All the way I felt sick in the stomach as a nervousness overcame me. I watched Mum's every move. The sound of the track and the smell of the smoke brought memories flooding back about the first train ride. I was so afraid of being taken away again. I was relieved to see Dad's happy face when he met us at the other end. He took us to Tighes Hill Technical College where he was the Greenkeeper Caretaker, and when he placed me on his tractor and took me for a short ride I forgot all about the train and the fear that had gripped me.

The same feeling of terror came over me whenever Mr and Mrs Reedman would bring me home after church in their car. I screamed and cried as I was afraid I was being sent away. I constantly kept Mum and Dad's car in view until we turned up the dirt track leading to home and then I relaxed, convinced we really were going home. Gradually with time I began to trust these new people.

Starting school was a whole new experience – as it is for any child – but I knew I was different from all the other kids. My skin colour was darker than theirs and if I forgot they always reminded me. It was a bit easier knowing that the Lynch kids were there and also the kids I knew from Sunday School. It was a small, one-teacher school with children in the classroom from kindergarten to sixth class. Wild Christmas bells grew all over the playground and I enjoyed sitting under the tall trees and watching the yellow-tipped red bells dancing happily in the sunlight. We never had these flowers at the camp so they were new to me. The other kids didn't take much notice of them, but I would rather watch them than listen to the teacher. Besides, whenever I did speak she always corrected me, making me pronounce my aitches and words ending in 'ing' to speak the proper way. I thought the way my grandfather spoke was the proper way. Our teacher was Mrs Sorbent and the children used to make fun of her; there was an ad on the radio at that time about Sorbent toilet tissue and the kids would sing the jingle out in the playground. I used to feel sorry for her as I knew what it was like. I now had a New Australian name and kids teased me about it.

To get to school I had to cross the train track, so Mum would walk me to the overhead footbridge, which was a quarter of a mile down from our house and regularly used by the miners going to the colliery. After school all the children crossed the bridge together and we soon learned to wait for the afternoon train and dared each other to run through the train smoke as it puffed and swirled up covering the footbridge to nil visibility.

Once, after having a good day at school and passing the courage test on the footbridge, I ran proudly home to tell Mum. As I reached the back door that led into the kitchen I stood frozen. I could hear the radio on in the kitchen. I couldn't believe my ears. I knew the song and it made me feel homesick. My heart pounded so hard I thought it would break. Tears dropped off my cheeks and I was so upset that I began hyperventilating. I was instantly transported back to the camp with my family. My grandfather played this song on his prized gramophone, and then later at night the uncles would strum it on their guitars while my mum and aunties danced around the campfire. Mum panicked. She kept asking, 'What happened? What's wrong? Was it the kids at school?'

'That song,' I finally blurted out. 'That's what my other mother played all the time.' I had no idea that the same song was now a very sad song for all the people at the camp as they too remembered the days when they played the song, when they were all much freer and happier.

BECOMING A FAMILY

It was three years later when I heard that song again. Most households didn't have telephones in those days, so you couldn't just phone the radio station and ask for the name of a song, but eventually we found out its name after Mum made numerous enquiries at record shops. It was called 'Joey's Song', by Bill Haley and the Comets. It was just an instrumental piece, a beautiful tune with no words. All budding guitarists try to pick it out. Mum couldn't obtain a copy of the record as it was no longer on the hit parade and unavailable.

My parents only turned the radio on to hear the news, so almost the only music I heard was gospel. Mum was in charge of the church choir and held practice at our place once or twice a week. It was strange how lots of things in this new house reminded me of life at the camp. Both my mothers had a love for music. They both had a good singing voice. They both played the piano accordion and they both sang me to sleep.

My dad was a very proud New Australian. He was a Yugoslav, but had fallen in love with Austria. He was Captain of King's Guard for King Peter. After the war, Dad decided to come to Australia to make a new start. Mum was born in Germany and came from a well-respected family just outside Munich. A trained opera singer as well as a schoolteacher, Mum had also decided to come to Australia after the war as part of the post-war campaign that invited Europeans with specialised skills to migrate to Australia to build a new life.

Dad was very committed to providing the best for his family. He bought many properties, made renovations to the houses and landscaped the gardens, then sold them, repeating this procedure until he had saved enough money to buy a small corner store; these were usually quite profitable as there were no shopping centres in the mid-sixties. My parents fostered me for three years and then signed adoption papers. After I was adopted Mum worked in Palings Music Shop, in the top end of Hunter Street in Newcastle. Here she was head saleswoman and knew her work well and found it rewarding, but after three years left her position to join in the business with Dad.

One could say I had adjusted to city life. I had no option. I loved swimming and as I splashed in the public swimming pools, I remembered the freedom of swimming in the river bank. I often thought of the camp on my birthdays, wondering what they might be doing or if they ever thought about me. At Christmas I thought of the white Santa man, whom the city children just called Santa. As the years passed though, it seemed I would rather forget about my first family, as I came to believe they had sent me away because they didn't want me. It made me so angry and resentful that I began to live in denial, putting my memories of the camp on hold from time to time.

My new family provided wonderful support for me, both emotionally and materially. I realise now that the reason they had such a good understanding of the racism I was experiencing at school was because as migrants they were also experiencing a similar form of discrimination. Both my parents had lost their parents in Europe by the time I was nine years old, so it was just the three of us in all the world and we came to need each other. They loved me, and I felt safe with them. Mum and Dad spoke German all the time to each other, and within a few years I could understand most of their conversation. I knew what I was getting for my birthdays and for Christmas. I was a quiet child, always thinking but not telling my parents many of my thoughts.

My new family was well known amongst the church community, and lived their Christian values at home. My father taught me what pride was and my mother taught me what loyalty was. We shared each other's joys and sorrows. I was their pride and joy. Their Christian love and faith demonstrated to me the commitment of real love and it was not long after a suspicious start on my part that we became a real family.

Lost

TEACHER'S WORDS

The major reason I enjoyed school was for the companionship with other children, as I pretended they were my brothers and sisters. Over the years I came to miss a lot of education as I attended many schools due to my father buying and selling properties which meant we often moved. Being transient also exposed me to the attitudes of people in different suburbs, but I found that although the suburbs were miles apart, the narrow prejudiced views of society were much the same. Society was ignorant in the sixties. Messages were repeated from town to town, from school to school. All I wanted was simply to be like all the other kids — white — but I couldn't pass the colour test. Nor could I say I was Aboriginal, as I didn't know one other Aboriginal person in Newcastle. I felt like I didn't belong anywhere.

So I couldn't claim Aboriginality, but was always stigmatised by it, always treated as a second-class citizen. Some teachers' comments totally demoralised me, such as, 'Oh, you darkies will never learn,' or, 'Why don't you go back to where you came from?' In the playground kids said, 'God only gave brains to the white kids, not to you.' Ajax was a powdered cleaning product, and I remember one year that not a week went past without one child saying, 'Why don't you take a bath and use Ajax, it washes everything white as snow.'

This was during the government's 'Keep Australia White' campaign when even the ads on TV and radio strongly reflected this attitude. Could anyone blame a child for not wanting to go to school in these circumstances? Before I could even see the teacher I had to make it through the piles of prejudice, racism and ridicule from both children and adults. What complicated it for me was that at all the schools I attended, I was the only Aboriginal person. I was the only child at home and I was isolated at school.

We moved from Whitebridge to South Wallsend where I attended first class. In the school playground was a cluster of trees where at recess and lunchtime, my favourite time, I built bark humpies and cubbyhouses with a couple of friends. This was the closest play activity to what I used to do at the camp with my cousins, but as I grew older the familiarity of it became more subconscious. I had about three friends who liked playing cubbies, and we had wonderful hours of fun just using our imagination. This kept us occupied for several months of the year, but I missed this outdoor activity very much during the winter months.

Once our teacher took us on a hike, a three-mile walk along a little creek that ran through South Wallsend past the Chinese market gardens. This creek ran through the end of the school property, over the dirt road and lost itself in the bush that covered a large hill. The hike was a real adventure and to this day, when I drive through what is now called Elermore Vale and see the little bridge over that run-off creek, I still remember that day when the land and environment became our classroom. That's how we always learned back at the camp.

Everyone remembers a bad day at school. For me it was the day when I wore a new dress to school. I had two new dresses, made out of cheap cotton, both identical, only one had large aqua dots and the other, large hot pink dots. In those days you had to wear your clothes for six months or for as long as they fitted. Apart from the special red dress, these were the only two dresses I owned and I was proud of them. We did have a school uniform for those families that could afford it but I thought I would wear one of my new pretty dresses and show it off. After lunch we did art. I was chosen to come out the front and sit up on a high chair and be the subject for a portrait. Some of the pictures were so exaggerated with my dark brown skin, black bushy curly hair plus the horrid hot pink polka dot dress that it turned me off wearing dots forever.

At this school, I first experienced a school fete which had every imaginable stall from arts and crafts, second-hand clothes, books, toys, food and raffles. After a barbeque lunch there was Scottish dancing, and I loved watching the kids dance between two swords. Then we had a grand parade where kids got dressed up and paraded their favourite toy. Some carried dolls, teddy bears, pushed prams, strollers or bikes. I felt like a princess pushing my old rusty stroller that Dad had decorated with colourful crepe paper, and I walked around the circle beaming with pride and waving at my parents.

After the parade at least ten kids came up to me and teased me something terrible about my dumb old pram. They said, 'Do you Abos get everything off the dump? It's probably filled with germs. You better have a bath tonight, don't bring them germs to school on Monday. We don't want to play with you no more.'

We weren't the poorest family at this school so I could only imagine what those other kids had to put up with. I cried all weekend. Half of these kids were at Sunday School the next day and acted like sweet little goody-goodies. I didn't want to go to school on Monday and during that week I was constantly reminded how dirty I was and how stupid the pram was. Lots of kids only had second-hand toys in those days, and to me my pram was the prettiest toy I had. If I had a brother or sister I could have shared these experiences with them, but instead I kept it all locked in my head, not even telling my parents.

From South Wallsend we moved to Waratah. Two doors up from our house in Dawson Street was the Gill family who had about five children. I was always welcome at their house, and the kids stood up for me at school so that the period of giving the new kid a hard time was chopped in half. I enjoyed being in a house where kids fought or played with one another, and I would come and go as I pleased. This family never mentioned the colour of my skin and I often thought they couldn't see that I was dark. I remember trying to work out how it was the Gill kids never went to Sunday School, but they had lots of fun in their house and always treated me kindly.

I attended Waratah Girls' Primary School. I found it was a lot easier on me just having girls and not having to worry about the treatment handed out by boys. At this school there were lots of rules to keep but not one particular teacher who made any special impression on me. I was losing out in my school work and falling further and further behind. Finally my grades became so poor that the school experimented with a plan which involved sending six girls from Waratah Girls' Primary School across the road to Waratah Boys' Primary School. Naturally I was on the list. The first week or two we felt so humiliated and hated being there. Then we felt embarrassed that the boys knew more than us, so we sat up and tried to learn real fast to impress the boys. Within eight weeks our learning had accelerated and we were well up with the average group. Learning became fun as we competed against the boys. We had been the guinea pigs and, seeing we passed with flying colours, were sent back to the girls' school while the next lot was put through the same system. We were all disappointed when we had to return to the girls' school, but I didn't have much time to readjust, as it was time for yet another house move. This time to Carrington.

I attended Carrington Primary School for third to sixth class. In fifth class I had a wonderful teacher, Mr McGregor, who all the children loved and admired; in fact, the whole school couldn't wait to be in his class. He was a born teacher who made each child feel important and treasured. Humour was his most valuable tool for educating children, and his room was filled with laughter. All the kids worked hard trying to please him as we respected him more than any other teacher at our school. We were very fortunate to be in his care for six hours a day.

One Monday morning in winter we arrived at school to be told that our dearly beloved teacher had died of a heart attack on the weekend, and it was like a part of our love for schooling also died. It always seemed like unfinished business, as he was there on Friday playing with us at sport, and then he vanished from our lives. Children were not allowed to go to funerals in those days so it was hard to accept the truth. Some of us pretended that he was still alive, just teaching at another school. It was probably just as hard for our new teacher to walk into our classroom as it was for us to walk in and accept him.

With each new school I felt like I was on trial for the first few months as far as the kids were concerned. I had to prove myself to them. Any child who has been moved from town to town and been the new kid at school knows of the power struggles that go on in the playground. By the time I entered third class, I had been through five primary schools, with my dad's buying and selling of property. These challenges in the playground did nothing for my self-confidence, and I hated the confrontation. I always seemed to team up with some other quiet shy child, and we tried to keep out of the way and let the leaders and followers play together.

Most of the girls from Carrington Primary School were going to attend the same high school, so that helped to alleviate my fears of yet another school. Their friendship was very important to me and helped me survive and socialise.

I was nine years old when I first saw an Aboriginal person in the city, on the television. I remember the night when Jimmy Little was on TV promoting 'Royal Telephone', the song that made him a household name. Mum and Dad were so excited and said, 'Look, there is one of your people. See how beautiful he is and look how the white people love him. This is your country, you be proud of it. We are the new Australians. Don't you be ashamed, you be proud you're Aboriginal.'

I was fourteen when I met another Aboriginal person face to face. I met Rhonda at high school but we didn't become close friends. We both observed each other across the playground. We probably had more in common than we thought. Although by my features people knew I was Aboriginal, within, I was in denial. I felt confronted. I had learned it was shameful to be Aboriginal, so instead of being happy to see her I was embarrassed.

At Wickham Girls' High School I found two teachers who showed me from day one that they accepted me without me having to prove myself first. They were my English teacher, Mr McGee, and my music teacher, Mrs Elkin. I worked really hard for them, gaining As in all my exams. I joined the choir to be near Mrs Elkin, and whenever sport was cancelled due to wet weather, I went to Mr McGee's classroom. He spent the afternoon opening up debate about subjects relating to teenagers, and then finished the lesson by reciting poetry. I remember the first poem he recited for us, it went on for ten minutes. It was 'Clancy of the Overflow'. Mr McGee didn't forget a word. It wasn't the subject matter that interested me, rather how it was delivered. This was the first of many poetry recitals and that is how I became interested in poetry.

Although I was quiet and shy, there was always a storm raging in my heart. I was hurting from the names I was called, and angry for being deserted and left alone without siblings. I found some escape by reading books and losing myself in the pictures and creating my own stories. I valued books highly, knowing from an early age not to draw in them or tear the pages. Books became my companions and

I found contentment in their silent world. I didn't know how to express myself verbally but my love for books and reading developed my confidence in written expression. Mr McGee, who always called me DP, which were my initials, encouraged the creative writing passion I had. Handing back an essay one day in second year, he said to me, 'DP, you are so good at composition, you must write a book when you're older.' So, Mr McGee, this one's for you.

I knew I was different to the other kids, however there wasn't much name calling at high school, as we were growing up together and starting to mature. It was great having friends like Deanne Wilson, Sarina Fracarno, Pam Jones, Kerry Mortimer, Mary-Jane Chambers, Annette Smith, Suzanne Porter and Glenda Smith. This was our group which sat together at recess and lunch for four years. We became teenagers, then young women together, and I felt accepted as part of that group. When we all turned thirteen and fourteen, it was a regular practice to all meet on a Saturday morning and go to the 'flicks'. It was winter, 1968, when I first saw a magnetic film that attracted me back fifteen times! The acting was excellent and the script even better. The leading male actor made such an impression on my young life that I still refer to that significant film today. It was the poignant, powerful *To Sir With Love* and the actor Sidney Poitier was to become my idol, hero and all-time favourite movie star.

In those days there was a silent acceptance of racism and prejudice, which wasn't even discussed, so this film was revolutionary for placing racism on the agenda for society globally. Sidney Poitier was the second black man I had ever seen in eight years, since being brought to the city. His courage and integrity gripped my heart. Three decades later

I am convinced that, although I didn't know it then, my starving Aboriginal heart must have leaped for joy and shouted within: 'He survived and you will too. Learn from him!'

All the girls used to rave on about their singing idols and movie stars, but they knew mine was forever the handsome Sidney Poitier.

School did not develop my identity as the curriculum didn't include Aboriginal perspectives or Aboriginal guest speakers, nor were Aboriginal people encouraged to become teachers. I often wondered where all the blackfellas lived and why I was alone. So seeing that inspiring man on the screen for two hours was the only black mentoring I had, and for me he was the world's best mentor.

FAMILY BUSINESS

At home, before and after school, I had to help my parents in their business, which was now a service station. I didn't mind, it was just a family chore that had to be done and it was fun. The service station opened punctually every day at 5.30 am and closed at 10.00 pm. We were driveway attendants. Personalised service in those days meant walking out to every car, serving the petrol, washing the windscreen, checking under the bonnet and putting air in the tyres when requested.

My parents worked so I worked. A family business meant working on the hottest of summer days and in the coldest of winter weather. Working in rain, hail and the annual southerly and westerly winds. We worked through thunderstorms, fog and the humidity of the summer season. Day in, day out, month in and month out, as well as year in and year out. Not only in good health but also when we were sick. We never took a day off or had sick days, let alone annual leave. We put in a sixteen-hour day, seven days a week for eight years. We had money in the bank but couldn't take a day off to enjoy it.

Being a driveway attendant was good exercise, all that walking all day long. I wasn't meant to work in an office, so the outdoor work suited me. We got used to the smell of petrol and the car fumes. We would serve over two hundred vehicles per day, and that meant talking to a lot of different people from all walks of life. The majority of people were friendly and there was only the odd one or two customers who thought they were upper class and you were the servant. We had regular daily customers from BHP, the dockyards and business people. We even had the regular holiday customers who would pull in only once or twice a year. They watched me grow up.

I suppose I understood why children were prejudiced and racist and just expected that when I entered the workforce I would be treated as an equal. But even there I came into contact with people who had negative perceptions of Aboriginals, as they (as well as myself) accepted the image the media presented about Aboriginals. If I admitted I was Aboriginal, the customers' facial reactions exposed their true thoughts, and so I soon learned if I said I was Maori or Fijian that this made me acceptable. My deepest desire was to be accepted, so it was easier to lie.

The hundreds of people we met every day assisted my communication skills with strangers. Locked away safely deep inside, I still had a lifetime of unresolved conflict concerning my identity, but I managed to fool everyone. I had no desire to trace my natural family, as it seemed with every passing year I had grown more angry about being sent away, and now I lived in denial.

Mum enjoyed the challenge of running a business but as Dad met his challenges he found it was time to move on. Dad prided himself on having the cleanest service station in town. I knew all the makes and models of cars and motorbikes. If we saw our customers at a shop or the bank we tried to match the car to the face as we didn't know everyone's name. I watched the young couples dating and becoming engaged and even saw some of them marry and have their first babies.

I knew the uni and tech students. I knew the surfies and speedway fans. We had regular customers in the RAAF and in the Army. I watched people going to church on Sundays and then go on a Sunday afternoon drive. It was interesting watching the world go by but I never felt like I belonged. In all the years we were in business I only remember serving one or two Aboriginal families but we had more Tongan and Maori families calling in. I suppose Aboriginal people were still living on missions and didn't have vehicles yet. It never crossed my mind that I should date an Aboriginal boy, just as the thought that I might marry an Aboriginal boy never occurred to me.

As BHP and all the other industries finished at four o'clock, our peak period was four to six each day with people travelling home from work. One afternoon a grey Holden EK pulled in for petrol. I stood beside the door patiently waiting for the driver to inform me how much petrol to put in the car. The four male teenagers inside were rummaging through their pockets and the glove box, searching between the seats and under the seats for whatever loose change they could find. Eventually they pooled their coins and had enough for one gallon of petrol which was exactly forty-two cents.

Drivers would watch me through the rear-view mirror waiting for me to signal that the required amount of petrol was in the tank and I would wave them off. I always felt uncomfortable knowing they were watching me. All the young boys in this car were looking and laughing at me so that I felt really embarrassed. Three years later my husband, Ron, told me that he was the driver and he had told his mates that day, 'I'm going to marry that girl.'

All my life I was chubby. I got used to Mum's European way of cooking and loved food. The boys weren't interested in me but were always interested in the other young girls we employed as casuals. Most of them were uni students and the part-time work helped them through their course as there wasn't AUSTUDY or ABSTUDY in those days. Dad was a tough boss, hiring and firing them quickly sometimes, but it gave me an opportunity to meet girls with varied personalities and just as varied goals for their future. Quite a few of the girls got dates at work and eventually this happened to me.

MEN WITH GENTLE HEARTS

One of the regular dockyard apprentices finally asked me out. My parents were very strict with me and I really did have a protected life, so when this young man fronted my dad for permission to date his daughter, Ron found he had to answer twenty questions and pledge his responsibility for my life. If he didn't already love me the way he did, he wouldn't have put up with all the conditions my dad imposed. I wasn't allowed to leave on my date until 7.30 pm and I had to be back home by 10.00 as we had to rise at 5.00 am so we could open the service station by 5.30. So the few short hours we had together were precious but restricted.

Our first date was to the cinema to see a John Wayne picture called *Cowboys*. In one scene one of the boys spoke in German and I was the only one who laughed as I under-stood what he said as my parents always spoke German at home. I couldn't speak German but I understood every word as I was a good listener. Ron said, 'That's not fair, you know what he said.' I was bored with the picture but I enjoyed the company and to be out on the town for a little while. Each time we went to the cinema we had to leave halfway through so I could be home on time. In those days when you went to the pictures you would see three or at least two pictures during a session, unlike these days when you only see one.

I felt embarrassed leaving early and not getting our money's worth, but if I was late I knew I wouldn't be allowed out again. If Ron wasn't genuinely interested in me he wouldn't have gone through the weekly routine of asking my father if he could take me out and being put through the third degree.

They say opposites attract and we did. My family was well off, his weren't. My family was Christian, his weren't, and I was Aboriginal and he wasn't. It seemed like we had everything going against us but Ron made me happy. I guess it was the rebellious streak in Ron that I found attractive, as he used to burn rubber whenever he pulled in and out of the service station and I liked his gesture of defiance.

Dad was not a man that you defied but Ron was his own person and this attracted me; there were so many things in my own life I would have liked to change but I didn't have the nerve, and I wished I was as strong as Ron. Of course he was very good looking and had sideburns all the way down his face with collar-length hair, not like the clean-shaven, short-back-and-sides boys at church. Ron's favourite jumper was brown with two orange stripes across the chest, and I knew our meeting was meant to be as that summer all my clothes were either brown or orange. I thought we would only date for a short time as I felt he was too good for me or, more to the point, I wasn't good enough for him.

We either went to the cinema or Ron's favourite spot, Heddon Greta Speedway, and then on Sunday nights we went to church. We did this for several months and grew to appreciate one another's company, plus it was my only time off work. Ron treated me like a lady and I liked being treated as if I was special, but I knew I was much less than special. It was strange seeing him burn in and out of the driveway squealing tyres and speeding going to work because whenever I was in the car he never did these things. I guess underneath my conditioned polite personality lay a rebellious daredevil spirit waiting to be released.

I was quite reserved. One night we parked the car on a hill that overlooked the lights of Newcastle and listened to the radio. Ron repeatedly asked me to look at him and tell him that I loved him. I couldn't. I was too shy. It was always difficult for me to express my emotions in words. I never believed that he truly loved me. I wasn't smart, I was over-weight, I was Aboriginal, and I wasn't worthy of his love. I had internalised all the messages I had received from society since I was five years old and knew only too well white people's expectations for Aboriginal people.

Just about every time we went out together Ron would say, 'I would love to marry you, just say the word,' but I never took him seriously. I thought it was a line that all boys whispered to girls.

Our birthdays were four days apart and Ron was two years older than me. I gave him a gold Ronson cigarette lighter and he gave me the most glorious diamanté necklace, bracelet, brooch and earring set. I couldn't believe my eyes when I unwrapped the delicate present. All I wanted was a friendship ring, this was too much. He was a first-year apprentice and I knew he didn't have that kind of money. He had been to every jeweller in Hunter Street not knowing what gift to buy. Nothing took his eye. Four hours later he walked into the last jeweller and spotted the set. His sister was with him and she kept saying, 'But, but . . .,' trying to say it was too expensive, but all Ron would say was, 'I don't care how much, that's what I want.'

It was dazzling. It sparkled like diamonds. It took Mum's breath away. She said, 'That is a special gift. That is a gift you would give to your fiancée, not a girlfriend. It is a very generous gift.' I wore it every time we went out. It looked magic when I wore it with a little black dress that had a fancy white collar, semi-puffed sleeves and a dainty little red rose on the collar. Ron loved that dress best, and would always say, 'You look a million dollars,' as the set dazzled in the moonlight.

Working for a living was a way of life and up until this time I had enjoyed work and the many hours it consumed, but gradually I found the work hours becoming monotonous. On the weekends I served the young couples with envy. How I wished I too could go on picnics, but that was not possible. For the next four months I felt like a captive, I became restless and longed for freedom. Marriage seemed to be an escape. When we finally became engaged Ron kept wanting to take me to meet his parents.

I was able to talk him out of it on several occasions, as I was afraid they would reject me due to my nationality. One evening he just drove to his house unexpectedly. They turned out to be very humble people who made conversation easily. As I looked around their home I could see they weren't well off. Apparently Ron's fear was that he couldn't provide for me in the way in which I was accustomed. His family had struggled financially all their life and had only moved from Limeburners Creek into Raymond Terrace six years previously.

Jack and Betty Meehan lived in Mount Hall Road. They were very friendly and made me feel quite relaxed. I found out all my fears about them rejecting me due to my nationality were uncalled for. Jack had worked with several Aboriginal men during his employment with the council. He told me stories about an Aboriginal man, Billy Widders, whom he'd worked with up around Halls Creek when they bulldozed the road over the mountain. Billy got up to so many pranks and kept the camp alive with his humour and escapades. Jack also told me about his father, Tom Meehan, who lived on the Barrington Tops, and he too had a long-time association with and respected the Aboriginal stockmen. It was a real education for me to see how easy it was for this poor family to accept me — nothing like I had expected.

Betty was a happy person, who said, 'I knew Ron had a girl somewhere but he wouldn't tell us who.' She offered me cups of tea and told me how they had four children and how hard it was to keep four children in the city. I think I realised that day that perhaps the reason my parents had money was because they only had one child to support. Betty had Aboriginal friends also living in Raymond Terrace and she convinced me that Aboriginal people were no different to them. I thought Ron's parents were all right and felt sorry for Ron that my dad had been so hard on him. As I sat on the broken-down lounge Betty held my hand

and told me they'd be proud if Ron married me.

The following autumn we married, on 28 April 1973. It was a budget wedding but for Ron all his dreams had come true. Deep in my heart I still felt I wasn't good enough for him. When I walked down the aisle and spotted Ron he was wringing wet, having broken out in a cold sweat thinking I had changed my mind and wouldn't turn up; he was also afraid Dad wouldn't permit it to go ahead. Ron's brother-in-law, Billy Boyce, was his best man and he chose his high school mate, Kim Whitworth, to be his groomsman.

I felt very feminine in my white wedding dress surrounded by the pink I'd chosen for the bridesmaids. Deanne Wilson was my bridesmaid, as we had known each other since first-year high school, and she was a quiet, sensible friend. Pat Jackobsen was my matron-of-honour and her five-year-old daughter, Elna, was my little flower girl. They were our Tongan friends and the three of us looked related as we stood together with our olive-coloured skin.

It was a small wedding with only seventy people attending, with ninety-five per cent of them being Ron's relations. At the farewell circle one of Ron's aunties whispered to him, 'Congratulations on getting married, dear, but you know it will only last twelve months, she is Aboriginal you know.' I suppose she expected I would go walkabout or something. Dad also wasn't happy with my choice of a husband; he felt I could have done better, which to him meant someone with a bank account. But he accepted that love is blind, and so we plunged into the deep with $100 left over after the honeymoon.

We spent our honeymoon at Katoomba. I remember how on our wedding night in the motel before we turned the

lights out, I read to Ron from the Bible, from the book of
Ruth.

> Don't urge me to leave you or to turn back from you.
> Where you go I will go and where you stay I will stay.
> Your people will be my people and your God will be
>   my God.
> Where you die I will die, and there will I be buried.

I had a youthful, romanticised idea of these verses, but
nothing could prepare me for the true meaning of those
words and how our life was to change.

TUBRABUCCA

My honeymoon was my first holiday ever. I felt like a queen not having to rise at 5.00 am. We spent three days viewing the Three Sisters, Jenolan Caves and the beautiful town of Katoomba. I loved the smell of the bush and on the fourth day we followed a walking trail that led to a waterfall. This was the first time I had seen a waterfall and I marvelled at its beauty and would have sat there for hours inhaling it all if I could. It was different to be wearing ordinary clothes all day long instead of my horrible green Caltex uniform. I felt free. I loved it. We also travelled through Sydney, and I never knew Sydney was so big, as it was the first time I crossed the Sydney Harbour Bridge.

On the fifth day we had to drive to Scone and meet Ron's grandparents, Mr and Mrs Tom Meehan. Ron had planned to meet his grandparents at ten-thirty at what they called Campbells Corner. We had a half-hour wait and then

Ron spotted their old green Valiant. An elderly man stepped out of the vehicle and strode proudly toward us. He was slim and tall, wearing an old suit topped off with a cap that sat slightly tipped to his right; altogether he displayed the steps of a dignified man. Ron stood just as proudly waiting for his beloved grandfather to cross the road to join us. As Ron beamed with joy I stood waiting anxiously, wondering if I would be accepted or rejected.

Grandfather and grandson shook hands and then embraced one another. Then the older man turned to me and as soon as he spoke I felt he was genuine and kind. Ron introduced me as his wife and then Pop, as he was known, gave me a reassuring cuddle and stated confidently, 'Welcome to the family.' I felt at ease. I liked him as much as I liked Ron's father and it was evident that Jack was a chip off the old block. I met Grandma over lunch and I knew she was the rock of the family, the one who carried her own problems and the problems of all her children.

We had a counter lunch at a hotel, the first time I had ever entered one. I knew Dad wouldn't want me to be there but it was different, I was with my new husband now. After a quick bite, we grabbed some supplies as the plan was to head off up the mountain to the grandparents' house. The grandparents had some business to follow up on and would only be half an hour behind us.

Within ten minutes of leaving town we were already in the farming district where the houses were further and further apart. This was another adventure for me and my first opportunity to see the Australian bush. For miles around all one could see were green rolling plains, grazing sheep and the odd farmhouse with smoke filing out of the chimney. The winding road was fairly wide, wide enough to pass logging trucks. I had never seen trees stacked on a truck before. I had missed so much, living in the city.

I noticed the black cockatoos that flew in great numbers and screeched ever so loudly; it was as if they were escorting us up the mountain and heralding the newlyweds' arrival. Along the roadside sat flocks of pink galahs eating seeds that had blown off trucks carrying wheat.

Once we drove through Moonan Flat the road became narrow and wound its way around the mountain with some steep descents. The bush was rugged and you realised you had to respect it. From the passenger side it was a sheer straight drop but I wasn't afraid as I had confidence in Ron's driving plus I was looking forward to seeing any kangaroos. Ron was very familiar with the road and talked about incidents where cars had overheated or rolled, but I only half listened as there was too much to see. I felt like Heidi going up the mountain to her grandfather's cabin.

Ron tried to prepare me for what lay in store by saying, 'Now don't expect anything fancy, it's just a few sheets of tin around a log cabin, nothing fancy, but I think it's beautiful.'

When we arrived two hours later, there was already a cold wind blowing and a fresh night was anticipated. The last hour's drive had been on a gravel road and the car was covered in fine pink dust. We pulled off what was called the main road and drove through a gate and grid that was kept locked at all times. From the main road it was a few minutes' drive through what looked like nothing more than a grass track and as we rounded a bend, there stood the grandparents' house, called Tubrabucca. I stood paralysed gazing at it. Ron must have thought I was disappointed at the sight but it forced me to remember something I had deliberately forgotten over the years – my childhood camp at Coonamble.

After we unpacked, Ron went about lighting the fire so it would be welcoming for his grandparents when they arrived. I looked at the old visitors' book and was surprised to see how many important people had stayed in this little cabin on the Barrington Tops.

It was a real education for me, staying with these country people. They were real pioneers of the Hunter Valley. We spent hour after hour listening to yarns and funny life experiences. Sitting by the fire was so relaxing and my mind kept straying back to another camp fire lost somewhere in my past. The men shared stories about the different vehicles that had got bogged in wet conditions or lost in the intense mountain fog. When each story ended it was time to put the billy on and make another pot of tea and then another story would proceed. There were stories about trout fishing at Hunter Springs, the Boggs, or Carey's Peak. Stories about the people who had lived on the mountain.

As we cooked tea together Grandma told stories about her various children but they were just names to me as I couldn't remember the faces from the wedding. She took me through the photo album and filled me in on the stories behind each snapshot. After tea we played a game called 'Sorry' but it took me a while to get to know the rules. In between playing Sorry, and making cuppas, the stories flowed just like the tea.

During the four days we spent at Tubrabucca my mind constantly roamed back to the days in the shack at the camp in Coonamble, and my tears were signs of the locked-up memories being released. I explained that the smoke from the fire made my eyes water, but it was the old corrugated tin wall with its thick layers of black smoke that kept whispering to me.

OUR FIRSTBORN

After our return from Tubrabucca we settled down to married life. I found the transition between dealing with hundreds of people each day to only seeing Ron very difficult, and boredom soon set in. Days on end I would never speak to anyone. We moved house a couple of times and eventually rented one of my parents' properties at Maitland, but this only made me feel more isolated. There were no young people where our old house was situated. I felt more and more trapped within four walls.

But when my firstborn came along I devoted myself to him, he was the centre of my world. My baby gave me great joy and it was the most wonderful thing to know that there was someone in this world who was totally dependent on me. I had Belinda chosen if it was a girl and Ron chose Darren if it was a boy, so Ron won. This baby literally meant the world to me as it gave me a purpose to be on this planet. This was mine and I treasured every moment with him. All I had ever wanted was a baby, and he was beautiful. It was something wonderful for me to look at my olive baby and see him laugh back, then in time crawl and walk.

I was quiet to live with. I wasn't opinionated, I didn't share my thoughts, even with Ron. I felt dumb and useless but I knew I was good at being a mother. Somewhere within me was the desire to prove to myself and the world that I could care for my baby and that no-one was going to take him from me. I guess it was the anger overflowing from being sent away that made me so determined to be a good mother.

Psychologists believe that the individual has an impact on society, whereas sociologists believe society has an impact on the individual, and for me this latter belief was so true. Although my beautiful baby kept me physically busy, emotionally I was retreating. I became withdrawn and pessimistic. Over the years I grew increasingly self-conscious, to the point of feeling inferior. I felt like society was watching me and had an expectation of me, not a good one. I felt I was more or less expected to fail. For instance, when I went shopping I noticed the stares people gave me, or the shop attendant keeping a watchful eye on me, as an Aboriginal person was always suspected of stealing. I did indeed feel like a failure and the need to be accepted was ever present in my thoughts.

As the years passed I felt lost and lonely. I only watched TV and visited my mum once a week. As time went by I was more convinced than ever that I really was dumb and stupid and only fit to wash dirty floors and nappies. When we had the occasional visitors, I sat nervously waiting for them to leave. I had nothing to talk about. I couldn't think how to make conversation. My heart murmured and the nerves in my stomach would tighten so much I had cramps.

In the first couple of years Ron struggled trying to provide for his family. Although he was now a tradesman, the dockyard was plagued by strikes and he made less money as a tradesman than he had as an apprentice. We never made up the lost wages. He did as much overtime as possible only to be taxed more and it was hardly worth the extra effort. Ron took his responsibilities seriously and worked twelve-hour shifts trying to make amends.

Dad died suddenly in July 1975. Before he died he had put the house we were renting up for sale, so with his passing we moved back home with Mum. We thought she would need support being left alone, and also it helped us out as much, as we were without a house. While we lived with Mum it enabled us to get on our feet.

Having a toddler around brought joy to Mum's life. She loved watching him walking and talking, buying him toys and going to parks. Living with Mum gave me the support I desperately needed, although neither Ron nor Mum knew how threatened and inferior I had felt during the past two years. I enjoyed going out shopping every day. I now had Dad's car to get around in and it helped to bring me out of my shell. Mum was a friendly person who talked to everyone in the street, and I gained a bit of confidence in communicating to strangers, but it was still very difficult.

We went to church on Sundays which I had missed since I got married. We had been married at Sandgate Baptist Church by Mr Ron Gibbins. Mr and Mrs Gibbins had a wonderful gift of hospitality and regularly had international guests staying at their house. I was really taken by this couple who seemed to find it so easy to love people from all races. I thought they were something special, as I grew up in a society that often cast you as inferior if you were different.

Ours had been the last wedding at Sandgate Baptist before the church was transported to Muswellbrook. Sandgate was a friendly country church and the congregation had watched me growing up from when I was eleven years old. There were two special ladies there who I will never forget. One Sunday night after church Mrs Gibbs said to me, 'Donna, there is something special about you. I don't know what it is but I know you will grow up to be a lovely young lady.' I always felt fat, dumb and ugly so her gentle words were like a healing ointment on my wounded heart. The other lady was Mrs Daph Nichols who was the most gracious woman I have ever met. She had the most beautiful speaking voice. Her eyes were filled with love. She spoke to me as if she had known me all my life. Mrs Nichols arranged the flowers at the church on my wedding day. She waited outside the church for Dad and me to arrive, and she gave me some hopeful, wise words about married life before I walked down the aisle. Mr and Mrs Nichols also took me to Singleton Aboriginal Inland Mission (AIM). The Nicholses told me that lots of Methodist and Baptist churches from all over NSW would mail large bundles of toys, crafts, books, clothing and blankets to the AIM and these were distributed to towns out west. At the Singleton AIM there were also a few Aboriginal families who were studying to go into the ministry. I saw a few Aboriginal families but I didn't meet anyone called Welsh, which was my mother's name.

At Sandgate Baptist everyone had felt like family. When we went to another, larger church for a few months after we married it wasn't the same, so we stopped going. I hadn't been to church for sixteen months until we moved in with Mum. She couldn't drive, so I offered to take her to church and found I enjoyed falling back into the usual Sunday routine.

MEANING TO LIFE

We lived with Mum for over twelve months but when I fell pregnant for the second time we had to find alternative housing, as Mum's house was only two bedrooms, and Darren was old enough to go into his own bedroom. In June 1976 we moved into a large three-bedroom home rented through the Department of Housing; when we married Ron had applied to the Department, because he wanted to provide for me. Mum would miss us all terribly but we wanted to establish our own home and raise our family.

But in late September, I ended up in hospital with a severe miscarriage. I was very upset with losing the baby, and I wept for hours on end. Broken-hearted and feeling so empty inside, I couldn't sleep at all that first night and started praying, which helped me focus. Strangely I became aware of a new strength and even a little hope. About four o'clock in the morning I made a promise to the Lord that I would become a Christian, and I allowed Him to take control of my life. Despite being raised in a Christian family, this was the night I truly became a Christian.

Even though now I was a Christian I wasn't given all the answers to the meaning of my life, and I didn't wake the next morning thinking I knew all the answers or even feeling like a brand-new person. In fact, I was still in hospital mourning for my lost baby, still feeling different to everyone else in the room, still angry and still poor. The only difference was that I had made a promise to the Lord, a promise I meant but didn't really know how to keep.

I suppose I thought I would keep my promise by living a good life, so I kept house trying to please others, trying to prove to white society that I wasn't dirty. For close to a year I was taking three showers a day, all to prove I was clean. I still felt inferior about being different, and I had an ocean of anger within me about many things in my life, past and present. I grew more lonely and miserable to the point where I wanted to commit suicide. Ron was working weekends and twelve-hour shifts trying to make ends meet but it all went on bills, rent, food, and paying off furniture and a reliable car. There wasn't any money to go out for a meal or a night out. We couldn't afford a second car and my isolation intensified my feelings of inadequacy and inferiority.

One day in November I seriously contemplated suicide. It seemed to be the only way out. I was boring and my life was boring. The more I thought about it, the more I convinced myself that Ron and Darren would be far better off without me. I didn't know exactly how but suicide would definitely be an escape. I knew I just wanted to end it all,

I wanted to die. My thoughts were interrupted by my three-year-old who came running in from playing outside. He ran over to the lounge where I was sitting crying and feeling utterly depressed and he proudly handed me a bunch of flowers and weeds he had picked from the garden and said, ''Ere are, Mum, I love you too much.'

I broke down and wept buckets of tears. It was as if he was sent in to distract my thoughts. It suddenly occurred to me that if I was to suicide it would mean my three-year-old would have to go through life without his natural mother, and that it would be history repeating itself. What was the meaning of my life?

I coped by taking one day at a time. The thing that let me hang in there each day was that I couldn't leave my baby alone in this big world. My firstborn gave me new life. I didn't have any confidence in myself due to the fact that I had no self worth. Looking back now it doesn't seem such a big deal, but I was a mess and each step I took involved lots of courage. If you asked me then what was the problem, I doubt that I would even have been able to verbalise it. It was an intense, lonely feeling, doubled by what was an emerging identity crisis. I had been living such a lie for so many years, I often thought I was living in my own bubble. Well, I suppose the day my baby brought me to my senses was the day the bubble burst.

First I understood I had to live to see my baby grow up and to be there for him whenever he needed me. It seems strange to say now that I loved my baby more than my husband, but as I said earlier, I didn't believe I was worthy of anyone's love, nor did I really believe that Ron loved me. I suppose I thought he only wanted to marry me for my parents' money and not for myself. Besides, Ron was a grown man and I was only concerned about helping a three-year-old through life until he was himself an adult. Anything less would have been mean and quite unmotherly; plus I certainly didn't want to desert my child as I felt my natural mother had deserted me.

I had very little information to go on about my natural mother, so all the attitudes and beliefs I had about her and my first family came from the few early memories I had stored in my subconscious. Even though now I can see the whole picture so clearly, the anger then inside me was really years and years of grieving that was never acknowledged, identified or resolved. The impact of instant separation had such implications upon my psychological development and my perceptions of the world around me that it took years before it manifested itself. It was exactly like an infected sore, left untreated for a lengthy period, and ultimately developing and infecting the whole bloodstream. I didn't identify the real issues that day in November, in fact real understanding of the true situation would take another five years. But for now I wanted to live each day for my child. I didn't want to let him down.

Now that we'd moved out of Mum's, I wasn't attending church again as I didn't find one that I felt comfortable in; plus I would have preferred Ron to be going with me, but that wasn't possible so I chose to remain at home. I would visit my mum once a week and spend the day shopping; apart from that we would visit Ron's parents every Sunday night, so that was our special night out as a family. I still didn't have self worth but I had enough will to live because I was now pregnant again.

Two months before Darren turned four I gave birth to

our second child, another boy, and I named him Tim after my father. I loved being pregnant as I felt like a real woman and I enjoyed motherhood immensely as this gave my life purpose and I planned to see my children grow into adults. It was hard work though, as Ron was on shiftwork and the second baby needed feeding every two hours, which was so demanding it exhausted me daily. I got so far behind in the housework but Mum lived on the other side of town and she couldn't come and help me around the house.

I also had to keep the yard because Ron worked every weekend. I didn't have an automatic washing machine or a vacuum cleaner, I didn't even have a mop. I washed the floor on my knees with rags. After months of this madness I wished I could go walkabout. I would burst into tears just trying to get the two boys ready to go shopping or to visit Ron's parents.

I didn't know the word 'stress' back then, but I was certainly stressed and frustrated; I could feel myself going backwards again. Ron insisted I continue breastfeeding, even though I wanted to put baby on the bottle, because he was convinced that mother's milk was best and that the baby wouldn't catch a cold, so I continued for the baby's health. I couldn't think for myself and so did what my husband said, as I always believed he knew better.

But Ron obviously recognised how stressed I was and he arranged a holiday in the country with his aunt and uncle in the Hunter Valley. This would be Darren's first holiday and, apart from the grandparents' fiftieth wedding anniversary in 1974 when we returned to Tubrabucca, it would be our first family holiday. I awaited the weekend eagerly, I so needed a change.

Going to Gundy

NO SHAME

We packed the car and set off after an early breakfast. The change of scenery revitalised me. I was delighted to be out of the four walls that imprisoned me. I once again felt that sense of freedom as we travelled through the countryside to a small town called Gundy, twenty minutes outside Scone. I was scanning the countryside trying to see everything that was happening. I noticed the different shades of green and the patchwork fields that the farmers were working on. I was captivated by the repeating hills and the flowing river that we continually crossed. My wish would have come true if we could have stopped for a couple of hours and just breathed it all in.

I wondered what it would be like staying with Ron's relations. If I hadn't been so stressed out I wouldn't have gone. Ron had introduced me to his aunt and uncle, Lorna and Vince Hayes, when we were on our honeymoon and we dropped in on our way to the Barrington Tops. It seemed like the house had been turned upside down. I wasn't impressed. The house was very old and needed painting; I had been used to Dad painting every house we lived in, so that when I saw theirs I was very judgemental. Spiderwebs had been left undisturbed for years. The house was filled with boxes from one end to the other and the kitchen was in a frightful state. As we drove away that day on our honeymoon I had vowed to myself I would never go back and visit them again.

After five short years in my house I realised to a degree what a lot of repetitive work housework was and how easily it could build up and look like a bomb has just been dropped, but I hadn't learned much really, so this trip was going to hold a lesson that I would carry in my heart for the rest of my life.

Aunt greeted us three hours later with a big squeezy hug and as I unpacked I felt grateful for the opportunity to go on this holiday.

Ron and his uncle strolled casually towards the giant old rusted shed towards the back of the block and as they walked off I could hear them discussing machinery. Four-year-old Darren followed the men only to be bowled over by the farm dog. The two soon became friends and teased and pulled one another with respect. They put in two hours of serious play. I kept a close eye as I wasn't a dog lover and didn't trust them. This dog was so gentle and obviously used to children throwing themselves at him.

I watched Darren as I sipped a cuppa in the old kitchen looking through the double open doors that led onto the verandah which went right around the house and had faithfully protected the old farmhouse all its life. As I sat in that country kitchen I politely listened to Aunt retelling the history of Gundy and the characters it had held.

As Aunt continued talking I looked at the ceiling, it was over thirteen feet high and hadn't been painted in twenty years. Not only had it not been painted but it was full of cobwebs. I tried to ignore it but I kept thinking of all the spiders. I also couldn't help but see the boxes filled with jumpers, magazines, old toys and material. What a hoarder, I thought. Aunt interrupted my thoughts by showing me her prized possessions of ornaments and gifts she had received over the years. She spoke about the numerous treasures she retrieved from the local dump and I was surprised that she made no attempt to hide the truth. I thought to myself how I would never do that, or if I did I would certainly never tell anyone.

She cooked a wonderful meal and I was so pleased I had got a day off from the kitchen. I helped Aunt dry up and put away the cracked, chipped crockery. She showed me how to pump water from the creek and how to use the old hand wringer in the open so-called laundry. Both Darren and I were so curious about the old outhouse. I thought, What paupers.

As we chattered in front of the fire on that first evening there was a knock at the door. It was a neighbour down the road who had had his electricity cut off and was worried about losing all his meat in the fridge. Aunt immediately replied, 'No problem. Bring it down in the morning and put it in my freezer for as long as you need.' The neighbour promised to give aunt half a sheep for all her trouble. After he left, Aunt sat down beside the fire and gave it a proud shove and confidently added, 'I picked that old freezer up at the flea markets for a song. I knew it would come in handy one day.' I didn't know what a flea market was and Ron explained what it was later that evening. I just couldn't dismiss it from my mind and I thought, How could she lower herself to go to such a place. Some people got no shame.

As we crawled into the bed that had two old mattresses piled on top of one another, I looked at the blankets made from patches and I whispered to Ron, 'She wears old clothes and she doesn't wear makeup or do her hair up,' half as a question and half as a statement. Ron said, 'She's lived a hard life on the land and the only time you do yourself up is to go to town for supplies once a fortnight. She's got nothing to hide. What you see is what you get.' Then I said, 'She talks so loud.' Ron explained, 'The only reason we talk soft in the city is because we don't want the neighbours to know our business – here you don't have that worry.'

I lay in bed thinking negatively about his answers and about all the things I had observed that day. I was worried sick about the spiders so only when I was drop-dead tired I forgot about them and went to sleep. I woke during the night and was so afraid of using the outhouse that I almost woke Ron to walk me out, but gathered enough nerve to go. I ran all the way back to the house and jumped into bed and pulled the blankets over my head. I had always been afraid of the dark but I had never told my husband. It took ages to get back to sleep.

THE HOUSE AT GUNDY

S omething woke me. It was daybreak. I lay in the soft, comfortable bed bewildered at what I had heard and waited for it again. When I heard it, I jumped out of bed and raced to the window. There was a gum tree, not fifty feet away from the house, and it was full of birds. I woke Ron and asked him what birds they were. When he understood the question, he mumbled, 'Just common old magpies or currawongs.'

I stood in my nightie at the window and watched them for ten minutes. As it was quite cold I crawled back into bed and just lay there with folded arms listening to the birds talking to one another. I had never heard them in the city. There was a magical beauty in their calls which sounded like music to my ears. The tears silently rolled down my cheeks as my subconscious released a trapped memory, and I realised they were the same birds and calls that used to wake me every morning when I was a child back in the tin shack at my grandparents' camp. I hadn't heard that sound since I was taken away. I lay in bed and listened and listened as my heart pounded and the tears became a spillway. I wondered what had happened to the people at the camp. Why hadn't they ever come looking for me? Were they still alive somewhere?

I knew Aunt had been up for a while as I heard her stoking up the fire and making a cuppa. She interrupted my thoughts as she entered the bedroom with a welcoming cup of coffee. It was a real treat to have a cuppa in bed and I thought she was so kind.

That day as I fed our baby Timothy, Aunt rambled on and on and I thought she could talk under water. After Aunt Lorna placed a casserole in the oven she scanned the hills through her cheap binoculars, which had also come from the flea markets. She exclaimed anxiously, 'The common's on fire!' Within five minutes she had saddled up her horse, secured her cowboy hat on her head and was off. It was hours before she returned. I thought women simply didn't do that and that she must be a tomboy. I mentioned to Ron that Aunt talked a lot, and he said that she probably hadn't had a visitor for weeks and appreciated the company.

As I waited for Aunt to come home I was kept busy with Darren and Timothy. Ron showed Darren and me the river that flowed directly beside the property and we spent half an hour skimming stones across the top of the water. It was great fun, the first time Darren and I had ever done that. After we collected some smooth stones we headed back to the farmhouse. Uncle spent most of his day with Ron talking about machinery and other boys' talk. Uncle Vince was sick with blood pressure and arthritis and wasn't able to work much, so he mainly poked around the house and did whatever he could.

As we neared the house we saw Aunt ride across the hill and come down to the property. Aunt was very thirsty when she leaped off the horse. She had been beating the fire with wet sacks until it was entirely out. It was very, very dry country, and a fire would have been a major threat, not only to livestock. After a thirty-minute break Aunt had other jobs to do, including visiting her neighbour across the road. She invited me to go with her, so we walked to her neighbour's house as she explained that this was where her daughter's mother-in-law lived.

The house was very dark inside and musty from being closed up. We found the frail old lady in bed with an ulcerated leg. She was ninety per cent blind and never left her bed, as she found it too difficult to move around. Aunt went over to her house each day to take her a meal, bathe her and change her dressings. When she was bathed and placed in a fresh nightie, Aunt spoon-fed her and told her the news of the day. As we walked back home I said, 'That's kind of you to take care of her like that.' She shrugged her shoulders and said, 'That's nothin, she'd do the same for me.' For the rest of the day I wondered if our own mothers-in-law would do that for each other.

Aunt spent an hour loading the freezer with the neighbour's meat and then prepared the evening meal. Later that evening as I stood outside under the stars I pondered many things in my heart. I had learned some valuable lessons. Although money had always been important to my dad and important to me, I had learned it wasn't that important to everyone. Money couldn't buy what this woman had. You don't buy kindness and charity — it's part of your spirit. I realised that her house was a mess because she was always out helping someone else in that tiny community, and that was a higher priority than housework.

Aunt showed me how to unpick jumpers and make new things out of wool, which she did for her daughters, Dawn and Nora, and her six grandchildren. I observed as she washed and repaired the old toys and made new clothes for them and sold them at the flea markets. She loved reading magazines and lots of books as they kept her stimulated and in touch with the world, and so she always had something to tell her bed-ridden neighbour. Aunt also made her own get well or birthday cards from pictures from old magazines.

Aunt must have noticed how discontented my baby was because she said, 'Donna, it's not the cow with the biggest udder that has the most milk. Give bub a bottle — it won't hurt him.' She made up a mixture of cow's milk and I gave Timothy his first bottle. He then slept for five hours straight and I was thrilled to have a few hours' rest, the first in seven weeks. The stress that had overwhelmed me had now gone, and I couldn't believe how much I had been trying to cope with.

On our last night at the little house at Gundy I happily gazed at the brown smoke-stained walls and the cobweb-filled ceilings and prayed, 'Lord, thank you for showing me how proud I am. Thank you for teaching me money won't make me happy. Bless Aunty Lorna as she has a heart filled with real love. Bless her home as its walls are silver-lined with love. Bring me back again. Amen.'

Whenever we could afford the trip we did return for a weekend holiday, and with each visit I began to love Aunty Lorna more and more. I had become more down to earth and even though I never said anything sarcastic before, I would think it to myself; whereas now I had learned humility and seen that I had nothing to be proud about. Some people might have called me stuck up; but either way, by 1978 I had well and truly fallen off my horse and was trying to live and raise a family just like everyone else.

Over the years our special visits to Aunty Lorna and Uncle Vince's place were times all the family looked forward to. As the boys grew up they loved the farm and its activities: playing in the river or riding horses, wrestling with sheep and goats. Most of all they loved the galahs and cockatoos that used to carry on conversations between themselves. It really was a boy's paradise. Uncle was still in poor health so he looked forward to spending time in another man's company. Of course Aunt and I never ran out of things to talk about. I wasn't a great one for talking but prided myself in listening. Aunt shared most of her life and experiences with me as we spent hours flicking through photo albums and learning her history from each photograph.

It is possible for a picture to paint a thousand words. I heard stories about growing up at Tubrabucca and how this woman found the courage to survive through the Depression, floods and the war. She showed me the futility of airs and graces and specifically showed me the true meaning of a community volunteer.

We went back to the little house at Gundy to celebrate Aunt and Uncle's 25th wedding anniversary with the family. Twenty-five years on the land. Hard years, but the hard years build character. It was lovely to see the old homestead filled with their dearest friends and to hear the old yarns again. Sitting beside the open fire and listening to the laughter made me feel warm, welcomed and at home.

DIAMOND FRIEND

It took me a couple of years to learn the routine of running a house but I was very flexible as playing with my children or watching their favourite TV programs with them was far more important to me. I loved motherhood and all the different stages my babies went through. I idolised them and wanted to give them the world.

The thought of going back to work never entered my mind as I wasn't skilled and still believed I was only meant to be a mother. And I enjoyed it. Darren was four and a half and Tim was born in August 1977. I had two beautiful, olive-skinned babies, both with dark brown eyes and thick, dark brown hair. Darren's hair was straight like Ron's and Tim's was curly like mine. Darren took his responsibility as a big brother very seriously and was good company for Tim.

By 1978 I had found a church home. I had taken my second baby to show an elderly woman, Mrs McIlwain, who had known me since I was six years old. She was such a loving person and she invited me to come to her church as I told her I wasn't comfortable in any I had gone to. I managed to get myself and my two boys there the next Sunday and found all the people very warm and friendly. I sat behind a lady in the back row. She turned around to see who the children were and when she saw me her eyes lit up and she gave me the biggest smile ever, so after church we introduced each other and she made such a fuss over me and my two babies that I felt very welcomed and couldn't wait to come back the next week.

My new friend was Julie Howard from Toronto. The church we attended was the Reformed Baptist Church in a little old-fashioned building in Grinsell Street, Kotara. These people were just like the people at Sandgate and they became my church family.

Apart from two friends from high school who I wrote to, Deanne Wilson at Singleton and Sarina Fracarno in Melbourne, Julie was the only other close friend I had. It was the type of friendship I had yearned for. I loved her like a sister. I finally had someone I could confide in and talk about women's business with and someone to go to the park along with our children. We had no idea of the extent of this friendship and over the years the quality of it deepened and enriched my life in a miraculous way.

Julie was instrumental in providing the vital link to this jumbled jigsaw of myself. As we worked together on my psychology her friendship became very precious to me. She wasn't like an autumn friend that was here for a season and then drifted away, but like a diamond friend, precious and rare. I nicknamed her Jewel.

A LITTLE VICTORY

I took Darren's first day at school very hard. It was so hard to let go of him. He sat in the headmaster's office as we went through an interview and the enrolment and he had these big silent tears dribbling down his face. As I walked away from the school pushing Tim's stroller I felt empty and sad, and I cried all the way home. I had never learned to deal with separation.

I was only home for an hour and missed Darren so much that I decided to take Tim for a long walk and pass some time. As I walked I felt like that little girl back on the train when I was five years old. When I got home there was a bunch of flowers wrapped up in pretty paper lying on my back verandah. There was no card and I didn't have any idea where or who they came from.

When Ron got home from work he said he didn't buy them. It wasn't until the next Sunday that I learned that

Julie had come to visit knowing it was Darren's first day at school and how hard that first day is for young mums. Apart from my seventeenth birthday bouquet from Mum and Dad, this was the first bunch of flowers that anyone ever gave me and I cried for joy. That's the type of person she was, always thinking about other people and their feelings and showing her love in actions.

I got used to walking Darren to and from school just as the other mothers did. I chose to stand alone back from the other women in the afternoon waiting for our children to come out. I listened to the various conversations of the women. Some had something to say, others just wanted to be heard. I felt awkward standing there alone and was always relieved to get back home again. I would slam the door and only then would I start to relax in the safety of my world. My nerves got so bad that I had to go to the family doctor one day to see what it was and he told me I had hypertension — believe me it is very real.

In fact, I had hypertension, early stages of agoraphobia and panic attacks. Visitors always made me nervous so I would pretend there was no-one at home. I had stopped taking three showers a day and instead was working through my panic attacks.

Darren had been at school for four months when one day I remember as I stood at that school gate I consciously smiled at one woman and said hello. I felt real proud of myself for speaking up first. This woman was a hairdresser and very popular. She was always happy and had heaps of different things to talk about; I thought she had an interesting life.

When I got home I couldn't stop thinking about how I actually spoke to a stranger. That was a giant step for me.

I'd had a victory. Nothing dynamite but it was a victory for me. I had made a subconscious decision that afternoon, that being, *I didn't want to be isolated any more.*

Boomerang Words

SPIRITUAL LOVE

One of the first things I did was go up to the public library, join, and take out a book to read. I couldn't afford to buy a book and I had such a yearning for knowledge. I hadn't read a book since I was sixteen, so there I was in the library walking up and down the aisle, not able to make up my mind what type of book I wanted to read.

Then I spotted a book called *Child Psychology* and I thought that it would be a good book that would help me be a good mum, so I brought it home. It took me two weeks to get through it. I read every page, 271 of them. Something wonderful was happening. I could understand most of the book. As I read along I was saying to myself, 'I knew that.' Or, 'That's what I think,' and so by the time I finished the book something I thought had been confirmed on just about every page, and I realised that I wasn't dumb after all. I had believed the kids at school and the teachers when they told me I was stupid or would never learn, but now I knew I wasn't stupid.

I had just read the biggest book in my life and I knew some of the things in it. I felt so encouraged that I took out another book. All my life I couldn't figure out why society treated individual people the way it did, so when I saw the title of this book I thought it was exactly what I wanted. It was called *Why Does Man Think the Way He Does*, though it wasn't about men as a gender, but about humans in general. However, this book was too clinical for me to understand, so I only ended up with more questions than when I began. That was the end of my visits to the library for a couple of years but I had learned something valuable about myself.

The anger from my desertion gave me such a compulsion that I knew I would be a good mother. The books gave me the confidence to do a good job and my mother taught me how to love a child. As most girls realise when they have their own children, their relationship with their mother changes and they view her through different, wiser eyes. Mum and I had grown closer since Dad's death in 1975. It was just the two of us in all of Australia. Mum kept very much to herself, only attending church, not even being involved with the Senior Citizens or any of those other social or volunteer groups. Our Friday shopping day was the highlight of Mum's week when she would see me, and even more special, in the school holidays when she would also see Tim and Darren. Mum was kind and loving and it gave her great delight — as it does any grandmother — to give her grandchildren gifts, toys, birthday and Christmas presents. She was very generous despite the fact she only had a pension, and I know if we were still in business Mum would have spent hundreds on the boys. Mum's belief is that money is only good when it is shared.

Our birthdays became special events and we both enjoyed watching the boys growing up. How Dad would have loved them and spoiled them. Mum told me that Dad dearly wanted a son, and they knew I was lonely and needed a brother, so when I was ten years old they made an application to adopt a second child. Then they got the shock of their life.

The Welfare Department in Sydney went through the file and had an in-depth inquiry into the first adoption. They questioned why they had wanted to adopt an Aboriginal child. Dad explained how he had seen a white lady with twins who were very dark, and the lady had explained that you could foster Aboriginal children. She gave Mum the address and said to write to the Aboriginal Children's Association in Sydney with all their details, and that the association would place their names on a list and would inform them when a child was available. So Mum wrote a letter requesting an older child as she didn't feel confident enough to take a new baby. At that time Mum and Dad had a one-bedroom house, and I had to sleep on the lounge. When the Welfare sent the inspector, Mum was worried they would be refused a child because of only having one bedroom. The man laughed and said, 'We have thousands of these children. We don't care if they sleep in the roof.' Mum and Dad continued to work hard on their little market garden in Whitebridge and were surprised and overjoyed when they had an immediate reply to their application stating that they should be at Broadmeadow railway station the following Tuesday, 22 April 1960. A lady from Welfare would meet them at 10.00 am and give them an Aboriginal girl aged five years old.

When they applied for the second child, the Department was puzzled by how quickly they were given the first child, especially as Mum was forty and Dad was fifty. The welfare policy stated that the cut-off age for males was forty-five. I had arrived on Dad's fiftieth birthday! The Department couldn't find out who was responsible for the blunder in red tape and told Mum and Dad there was absolutely no way they could have a second child.

I was fostered for three years and then my parents signed my adoption papers when I was eight years old, as I had settled in. Church people would always ask Mum if I was fostered or adopted, and Mum would proudly say, 'Yes, Donna is adopted.' She would smile and look at me and say, 'That's not a secret, is it, Donny?' The kids in primary school tried to make adoption sound like an awful disease, and teased me about it, but it didn't worry me as I always felt safe and secure.

Even though I always knew the truth, it was good having Mum fill in the finer details. When I was older we had a special love for one another and I felt we were a lot closer than many natural mothers and daughters. It didn't matter that my skin colour was darker than hers, she loved me like her own flesh and blood. Our love was strengthened by a spiritual love. Mum was a real Christian, and she always showed me by her life, actions and prayer what true love was. It was a miracle that the Lord had chosen me for this home.

Mum also echoed what Dad had said many times, 'When the time is right, Donna should find her people, that's only natural.' My husband also repeatedly told me to try to trace my family history, but I didn't want to. I was afraid of what I'd find. I didn't want to offend Mum and Dad, I didn't want to confront the past. Ron was saving money so that when he got his long service leave he would be able to take me back to Coonamble to start searching for my mother and my brothers and sisters.

As I didn't believe we would ever have enough money I wasn't threatened, and life went on.

BOOMERANG WORDS

I was just a mother-in-training with my first child, and so was much more confident when my second child came along. Mum had remarried and was happy with her new husband, Neil. Mum continued to give loving advice, plus I had some wonderful women at church who gave helpful hints, shared books on parenting and even passed on children's clothes to my boys, for which I was thankful, as I couldn't afford to buy them. I was humble enough to accept second-hand clothes but I wouldn't dream of going to an op shop, as I thought they were for poor people. I know now that I was poor enough to go there, but at the time I was too proud to admit it.

Julie had two boys the same age as mine, so we had lots of things in common to talk about. We would go to the park in the school holidays and discuss the progress of our children. We shared books and clothing, we prayed together when we had problems, and it was reassuring knowing I had someone to confide in, to laugh with and to cry with too.

Ron and I were renting a three-bedroom brick house through the Department of Housing. It was thirty years old and the carpet, an old industrial striped one, was disgusting. We couldn't even dream about replacing it, so whenever I had visitors I was truly embarrassed about it, plus the old curtains that hung in every room in the house. It was hard saving enough money to pay the rent and put food on the table; I didn't have extra to spend decorating the house.

But Julie kept telling me, 'Don, I don't care what you've got in the house, I come to visit you.' I had known Julie for approximately one year. Julie always said she thought it was wonderful that I was Aboriginal. She knew quite a few Aboriginal families living in Toronto where she lived.

When I became a Christian the Lord had to do a lot of work on me, changing over twenty-one years of negativity into something constructive and positive. I learned that if we don't hear what the Lord is saying to us He always uses somebody else to help deliver the message. That is why he put Julie in my path. Julie always wanted to talk about where I was born and to hear about my life, but I didn't want to discuss it, especially about where I was born, I just wanted to forget that part. Ron knew it and now Julie knew it. Over the year we had been friends Julie had picked up on a couple of important things, and one day as we sat in my lounge room the conversation became very deep.

As we sipped a cuppa Julie asked, 'Don, you don't like being Aboriginal do you?' Guiltily, I shook my head. Julie went on to say, 'God made us all different. If He wanted a bunch of robots He would have made us all identical. You are special. Aboriginal people are special, and if you can't accept the way He made you, you're really saying God made a mistake, but God doesn't make mistakes.'

I brushed her words aside, but deep down my heart was pounding.

After Julie went home I sat on the lounge for one hour, tossing her words around in my mind. At first I felt guilty. Then I was angry with my natural mother for deserting me. I thought: I don't want to know them. I hate them. I hate being Aboriginal. Life would have been much easier if I wasn't. Then Julie's words would echo again. This argument went on and on until my spirit broke, and I wept. I had to face the truth. I said to my heart, 'It's true. I am Aboriginal and I can't run away from it any longer. I accept I'm Aboriginal.' I couldn't pray at the time, I just cried and cried. The ghost of denial that had shadowed me all my life had left. Finally, I was exhausted from crying, but I felt the weight that I had carried for over twenty years had gone. I also knew something excitingly different now stirred within me, although I couldn't identify what it was.

I must have looked a sight when Ron returned home from work that afternoon. As he greeted me with a kiss he asked, 'Why have you been crying?' As usual, I couldn't express my emotions. Then the tears swelled up inside again like a great tidal wave, and I said, 'I'm Aboriginal.' He offended me when he burst out laughing, saying, 'I know that.'

As we stood in the kitchen hugging, he must have thought I was mad. It had taken over twenty years for me to work out what the problem was. The problem wasn't that I was Aboriginal, the problem was that I didn't want to accept that. For me it was like a sunrise. Reality had finally dawned upon me.

HEALING A WOUNDED SPIRIT

Believing that God loved me, made me and, on top of that, thought I was special, took quite some convincing. I grew up believing society's opinion of Aborigines, that we were the lowest on the social heap, so I had always asked, How could God love me? I was unworthy.

But now, each time I read my Bible I found lots of promises that filled my days with hope. My minister, Don McMurray, taught me how to claim each verse for myself, so I would read, for example, 'Donna, I have loved you with an everlasting love,' or 'Donna, you are the apple of my eye' (Deuteronomy 32:10), and slowly, very slowly, I began to believe it. These were my first steps in faith. It was humbling to think that He who had created the stars, performed miracles, healed the broken-hearted and set captives free could possibly have time to be interested in little old me. This just blew me away. It was wonderful to know I had someone to listen to me twenty-four hours a day.

God was working on my insecurity. Between Julie and reading my Bible, I received lots of positive messages that began to heal my wounded spirit. I didn't know my Bible as well as Julie did so I studied it diligently. I had many lessons to learn and I enjoyed this new way of thinking.

I had been attending church for over sixteen months when one day in 1979, Julie invited me to a Christian Women's Convention to be held in Toronto the following Tuesday. When she asked me, I felt guilty as I hadn't read my Bible for two weeks and I really didn't want to go to the meeting. I made up an excuse, so Julie said she would ring my neighbour the next day to see if I'd changed my mind. When we spoke on the phone the next day I was still making excuses and said, 'I don't have a car, plus Tim is eighteen months old and I won't leave him, plus I don't have any money.'

Julie replied, 'Oh Don, I would love to pick you up and bring you home after. There's a crèche, you don't have to get dressed up, and you won't need any money. It will be just lovely.'

I walked back home cranky for letting myself be talked into something I didn't want to do. All my life I allowed people to talk me into things, as I wasn't confident enough to speak up, plus I didn't want to offend people. The word assertive wasn't used much in those days, and although now it is a popular concept, I find it is still difficult for me to be assertive. That's not from our culture. Even today, Aboriginal people are agreeable for the sake of it, but they should only agree if the heart agrees.

As I climbed into bed my last thought was, 'I don't want to go tomorrow.'

THE APPOINTMENT

Julie arrived on time the next morning, tickled pink that we were going to spend the day together. When we arrived at the community centre in Toronto, Julie showed me where the crèche was upstairs; we stayed with the little ones until they were settled, as I had never left my children anywhere before. Tim and Julie's son, Jonathon, were the same age, eighteen months old. We went back downstairs and, feeling lost, I headed for the toilet. Hiding there from the crowds of women, I was angry with myself, thinking I should be at home doing housework, as I'd left the house in a mess what with getting my kindy kid off to school, and having Tim and myself ready by nine o'clock. I was nervous and angry besides, thinking, 'I haven't been reading or praying like these women here.' I didn't belong here.

I hadn't expected so many people. So many strangers. There was quite a line of women waiting to go inside the hall. When I rejoined Julie, I did what I'd always done and allowed other women to go ahead of me. One of them was Aboriginal. We waited patiently in line. The hold-up was because each woman had to sign the visitor's book, giving their name, address and stating what denomination they were.

When it was my turn to sign the book, I had a quick stickybeak to see what the Aboriginal woman's name was. It read Margaret Welsh. I got a shock. My heart raced. I had always known the name of my natural mother, which was Beatrice Margaret Welsh. As I somehow walked into the hall and took my seat in the back row, I thought, Could that be my mother? As I sat down, I tried to remember my mother's face, but I couldn't. I recalled she was very dark and a big woman, and this woman was fairer and of medium frame, but perhaps everything looks big to a five-year-old. Could this really be her here in Newcastle? I kept trying to look at her, although she was seven rows in front of us.

Julie asked, 'Don, do you know that woman?'

I replied, 'She's got the same name as my natural mother.'

Julie nearly leaped out of the chair. She was ecstatic. 'Oh really! Go and ask her.'

But I was glued to the seat. I didn't want to. My hands were shaking. I was too shy to go up to her. Julie asked how I knew her name and I told her how I looked in the book. She put her hands over her mouth, she was so excited she wanted to yell it out, but a thousand thoughts fled through my mind. Just then the meeting started.

Rose Trousis opened the meeting, welcoming all the women. There were over a hundred and fifty women there. Rose was a real lady, I thought. She was tall, slim, well dressed and spoke very gracefully in a lovely sweet voice. I thought she was real elegant. She opened the meeting by saying, 'Ladies, you're not here of your own will today, you're here because you have an appointment with God.'

My heart was pounding as I listened to her words. Above her lovely auburn hair hung a sign saying, ALL ONE IN CHRIST. Rose was now praying and her words came through the microphone, 'Lord, some of us have been rushing around like mad this morning, quiet us. Some of us don't want to be here, bless us. We have come from different walks of life and we say thank you that we are all one in Christ Jesus.'

I was sure Julie could hear my heart pounding like a drum. We sang 'Great is Thy Faithfulness'. Then there were a couple of items where one woman sang a hymn and another gave her testimony, and then there was a time of prayer. After another song it was time for morning tea. We headed straight to the crèche to check the boys and after spending five minutes with them, we joined the women outside for a cuppa.

Julie was nudging me to go and speak to the Aboriginal woman, but I waited until the last possible moment. Inside the hall I could hear music signalling that the next session was about to begin. Nervously, I walked over to her and said, 'Excuse me, what's your name?'

'Margaret – Margaret Welsh,' she said softly.

'Where do you live?' I asked shyly.

'Cardiff,' she said with a smile. 'Where do you come from?'

'Edgeworth,' I answered.

'No, I mean before that,' she said curiously.

As I hesitated trying to work out which suburb to say, she interrupted and asked, 'Where were you born?'

'Coonamble,' I replied.

Then she told me she was from Walgett. I was looking at the ground thinking, it can't be her.

Then she said, 'Walgett is just up the road from Coonamble, you know,' as if she knew I didn't know where Walgett was.

All I could mumble was, 'Oh.'

'I've got lots of relations in Coonamble, you know,' she said in her quiet, soft way.

By now, all the other women were filing back into the hall for the second session. As I placed my cup on the table provided I finally asked, 'Do you know Beatrice Welsh?'

Her eyes lit up. She smiled proudly and said, 'She's a lovely person, that Beatrice. She's my husband's aunty.'

WHO WOULD HAVE DREAMED IT?

I was stunned. I think I felt relieved, and yet I still wasn't ready to meet the truth. All these years it had just been a name. I stood silently looking at the ground. I couldn't think of a thing to say. My heart was racing, and I knew this woman was looking at me, but I didn't know what to say next. I didn't know how to put it into words.

Cautiously, I finally whispered, 'Um – well, I think she's my natural mother.'

Margaret asked, 'What's your name?'

'Donna,' I said.

'Donna? Oh Donna! I know who you are now. We bin lookin for you everywhere. We gave up. We thought we lost you for good. My husband got all them boys home, you know. That old fella won't be believin me when I tell 'im who I been talkin with today.'

I was a bit lost in the conversation, as she spoke so softly.

I didn't know who the old fella was, or what boys she was talking about. After a brief smile, I went back to the meeting, not concentrating much on what was being said.

So she was my aunty. I retold the whole conversation to Julie, who was so overjoyed she nearly shouted for joy. She couldn't stop smiling. I was sort of happy about the news, but I was unsure and uneasy about a lot more.

Before we left that afternoon I wrote my address out for Margaret. I learned she attended the Church of Christ at Cardiff, but I forgot to get her address. What a day. Julie kept asking questions on the drive home. She said, 'And you never knew her, you didn't know you had any relations in Newcastle.' I felt strange having relations. Fancy them living five miles away from me, and I never ever saw them.

If I hadn't gone to that meeting I would have missed out on one of the most important days of my life. Who would have dreamed about it? I'm glad I got talked into it now, but I still had too many fears to realise it then.

What, for a start, would I say to my mum? How could I tell her?

Minya

UNCLE CYRIL

When I got home I kept thinking about Margaret and the strange meeting. I'd had no intention of going to it. I tried so hard to get out of it, even lying. A part of me was glad, but my mind was clouded with questions. Ron was a mixture of surprise and disbelief when I told him the news. After tea I went to the shed to be with him as he repaired a car, and as we talked a white 66 Holden sedan pulled up at the front driveway. We didn't recognise the car until a big, tall dark man got out from behind the wheel and waved to us. 'Oh no, here they come already,' I said to Ron. I hadn't expected the relations to visit just yet. The man walked quickly down the driveway, smiling and shaking his head in wonder. 'Look, Mum, she looks just like Beatie.'

It was Uncle Cyril, Margaret's husband. He had brown skin, but not as dark as his wife's. He gave me the biggest bear hug, then beckoned Margaret out of the car; following her were their children, Glenn, Bertram, Nigel and baby Brenda. I led them all inside and our children played together with the Matchbox cars. I sat and listened to Uncle Cyril talking about the family, mentioning names I'd never heard before. Margaret sat quietly, smiling and softly saying every now and then, 'This is lovely.' I was drawn to her quiet nature, and I sat admiring her silky dark brown skin.

As we had a cuppa, Cyril kept talking and making jokes. He told me how he tracked down all my brothers and took them home when they turned fifteen. Apparently, you could go to Welfare when you turned fifteen and they would tell you where you came from. Cyril was telling me how my mother, Beatrice, had another four children after she lost us all. It was a strange concept for me to believe I was not alone but in fact was actually one of eleven children. Cyril rattled off all their names but I couldn't remember in what order they were born.

Margaret looked at me, her brown eyes gentle and loving, and said, waving a little floral hankie, 'That them Welfare told us you went to New Zealand, they lied to us. We never knew you was 'ere in Newcastle, we would 'ave come long time before this.' As for Cyril, it seemed like he wanted to talk all night, though I wasn't much for talking in those days. He described this one and that one of my siblings, who married whom, who was this aunty's child, and who had died. He said, 'Your boys look just like Widdy's eldest boy.' I know he was thrilled to pieces to have found me but in the end I was feeling a bit threatened.

Before they left, Cyril placed a piece of torn paper in my hand. It contained Beatrice's address, and he said, 'You write to her tomorrow. She'll be dying to hear from you.'

I went to shake his hand, but he insisted on a hug. Seemed like in those days I had my own little invisible picket fence around my body, as I didn't like people getting too close to me. I felt like I was being suffocated. I was so tired by the time my visitors left. What an emotional day. As I slipped into bed my last thought was, Should I write or not?

Mothers' Day

The next day I telephoned Mum at Beresfield to tell her about meeting Margaret and Cyril and that I knew the whereabouts of my natural mother. I wept as I spoke, as I didn't want to upset her, I loved her too much and I didn't want this new information to affect our relationship.

But I could hear in her voice that she was happy to hear the news, and she reassured me that if Dad was still alive, he would be happy too. She reminded me how he had said, 'When the time is right, Donna must meet her family, it's only natural.' Mum and I cried over the phone together. She closed by saying, 'You get to know your mumma and brothers and sisters. I bet they're a big family and maybe one day, Donnie, I'll get to meet her. We just thank the Lord for this miracle. It's His will.'

The small scrap of paper with my mother's address lay in a blue glass bowl on top of the TV for a week. I glanced at it now and then. I tried ignoring it. If the boys chased each other through the lounge room the breeze would sweep it out of the bowl and onto the floor. I had so many questions. Who was she? What was she like now? Would she want to meet me? Did she ever think about me?

As I did things like wash up dishes I thought, Where was she when I turned twenty-one or when I had my babies? Why did she give me away? Was she a drunk, or worse? If I made contact would all my relatives start hanging around? Ron and I were private people, we kept very much to ourselves. As I hung out clothes, I wondered what Ron was thinking. Would Mum get offended? Ron didn't give me any answers, he just replied, 'Well, why don't you write and find out?'

The following Sunday was Mother's Day so I decided to write and let her know I was okay. I bought a nice card with a single red rose on the front, and included a three-page letter with details of our wedding, the boys, my parents and my childhood. I began the letter, 'Dear Beatrice', as I couldn't call her Mum. Too much water had gone under the bridge for that, in fact twenty-three years of flowing doubts and rapids of anger.

Beatrice replied a week later. She had been away in Walgett. Her son Robby had brought her the letter over from Coonamble on the Saturday. She wrote that my letter was the best Mother's Day present she could ever get. Her letter was filled with information, such as that Ron and I were married on her birthday, how my brothers all came home, and what my sisters were doing. She wrote: 'The government took all you kids away. I lost all seven kids that day. It was so terrible. They put the eldest five on the train and kept the three-month-old twins at the hospital.'

I knew we had twins in the family. I remember one day I was hungry, and instead of waiting for lunch, I opened up a large tin of powdered milk and ate half of it. I got into trouble when Mum found out, as it was the babies' milk. It so happened that that night there was meat and we had a barbeque. The smell of meat cooking surrounded the camp, but as punishment for being greedy, I wasn't allowed any. Luckily Aunty Tam quietly passed me some cutlets that had a mouthful of meat left on the bone.

Beatrice closed the letter by asking, 'Could I please have some photos of your wedding and Ron and the boys?' I was happy reading the letter, but part of me said, 'If we just write now and then, and they all stayed in Coonamble, I could handle it.' I needed to walk through my anxieties at my own pace and to do things in my own time.

LEARNING TO ADJUST

Beatrice and I wrote to each other for three years. I read between the lines and felt something wrong when her letters came six months apart. I thought she was going through a guilt trip. There was no depth to the letters.

I shared the first few letters with Mum as she was interested and then selectively, with sensitivity. We only had one small conflict over the letters, and I knew it was just as hard for Mum to adjust as for me. No doubt Mum had her own concerns, and I'm sure so did Beatrice, and I knew I had many feelings to deal with. All three of us wondered about each other. When I felt tense on one of my shopping visits with Mum, I went home and wrote her a letter saying how I loved her very much and how I would not forget all the things she had done for me. Life eventually got back to normal.

I was also growing as a Christian in these three years.

Learning lots of lessons about humility, learning to accept and love the poor. I learned how to take all my feelings to the Lord. Feelings of anger, sadness, confusion, stress, impatience and jealousy. It was beaut having someone to go to with problems, and knowing I could leave them with Him and walk away free. Free to get on with life.

During the five years since I'd become a Christian, the Lord had been working on my personality. He taught me how to think positively. He taught me how to speak. I used to have a loud, butch voice, but He showed me how to speak softly like a lady. Then He gave me a sense of humour to balance everything out.

I loved Sundays and going to church to worship. There were some lovely families there and I learned so much from the women. Although most of my learning came from observing, gradually, when I gained some confidence, I applied some of the things I had learned, and so I began to develop some communication skills. I mainly agreed with other people's opinions as I didn't have any of my own and still lacked a great deal of confidence. I was given a job at church writing to those who were sick or absent, and I enjoyed this, as it wasn't face-to-face communicating. I soon learned how to express myself in words, and discovered that lots of people enjoyed receiving my mail.

When our minister and his wife, Don and June McMurray, went to New Guinea for three years' missionary work, I missed them dearly as they had shown me so much love and taught me so much. June had asked me to take on her scripture class at Hillsborough Primary School while she was away, so communicating to little children became my training ground and gave me new confidence.

So I had been very busy during those three years. I had

needed space and time to evaluate the new direction of my life, as well as come to terms with my identity. I felt like I was sitting on the fence observing two cultures, trying to make up my mind which one suited me best.

THE UNEXPECTED VISITOR

It was the first Saturday in December 1982. The boys and I were busy on the lounge room floor making paper chain decorations for Christmas. Darren was nine, Tim was five and my third son, Mark, was eighteen months old. Ron had left the house as he had some casual weekend work in a truck depot about eight miles away. He had only been gone for ten minutes when there was a knock at the back door and I thought he must have forgotten something.

I opened the door to find a stranger, a very pretty young girl about seventeen years old. Stepping backwards, she said, 'There's someone here to see you.' A large, dark lady who had been hiding behind the house stepped forward into view. It took a few seconds for me to realise who it was. It was Beatrice. I recognised her from a twenty-year-old photo that Cyril had given to me.

I met her with a smile and gave her a quick hug and a

kiss, and did the same for the two young girls waiting behind. There were several people I didn't know. As I showed them into the house along our back verandah, Beatrice said, 'This is Jayne, Kim, Ken, Rachael and Shane.' I knew who they were from all the letters over the years. Jayne and Kim were my sisters. Jayne was one of the twins. Kim was always known as Tom, and was about ten years younger than me. The six-foot-tall man was Ken, Jayne's husband. I was glad he wasn't Aboriginal as I knew he and Ron would have something in common. Rachael and Shane were Jayne's two children and looked about the same ages as my two eldest boys.

The timing was perfect for more than one reason. Firstly all the children sat on the floor and made decorations together, but, more importantly, I had been given three years to prepare for this moment. You don't know how you will react at such a time. You make a plan and think you might say this or do that, but because you're not ready or not expecting it, the heart just takes over, which is the way things should be anyway.

As we sat down the clock chimed nine. Usually I would still be in my old dressing gown, but for some unknown reason I had decided to get dressed at eight o'clock. I felt guilty that I hadn't done the breakfast dishes, but it made my guests feel at ease.

My first question was if they wanted a cup of tea. They had just finished brekky, so they refused. I apologised that Ron wasn't there and explained how they had just missed him as he had left for work. I told them that Ron would have loved to have met them. I was able to speak in a soft voice and smile at the same time, because I learned how to do this from watching Julie. My visitors might have thought that I was confident but inside my body was shakin' all over, just like the song says.

The children occupied themselves on the floor. After a pause I asked, 'When did you get here?'

Beatrice replied, 'We travelled all night and arrived at Cyril's at 2.30 am.'

I asked, 'Where are you going?'

Kim giggled and said, ''Ere,' in a 'don't you know' voice.

I'm sure that in between the conversation we were all checking out one another. They seemed nice enough. Kim was very pretty and had a persistent giggle that made me laugh and helped us all relax and be comfortable. Jayne and Ken sat on the lounge listening and not interrupting. I didn't want them to feel left out so I asked them how you got to Coonamble. All four voices replied at once, and I heard places called Gulargambone, Gilgandra, Dunedoo, Sandy Hollow, and I thought, Wow, they really do live in the outback.

I felt at ease with them. Beatrice and Kim sat opposite me at the dining table, and as I looked at Beatrice I thought, I have never seen such a dark person before.

Then she said, 'Happy Birthday for last Thursday.'

I said, 'Oh, thanks.' I was surprised she knew or remembered.

The children's voices tied together the pauses. Beatrice commented, 'Darren looks like Jaimie.'

Kim looked and smiled, nodded her head in agreement and said, 'Mmmm.'

I knew that name so I said, 'Oh, that's Waddy's son.' Everyone, even the children, burst out laughing. 'Widdy,' they corrected me.

Making light of it I said, 'Oh well, I was close,' then I

asked, 'How long are you staying?' and Beatrice replied, 'We all goin home tomorrow.' The children were a helpful distraction as we all tried to think what to say next.

There were a million questions to be asked. There was, of course, the obvious and I was bursting to know, so I had to ask it:

'Why did you give me away?'

Jayne and Ken stood up and went outside for a quick exit under the pretext of having a smoke. The silence was deafening. The children, as if on cue, stopped talking. Beatrice hung her head as her eyes welled up with tears.

She said quietly, 'I dunno, they just took youse all away. I dunno why.'

That was strange, I thought. There must have been a reason. Everyone was deathly still and I knew I could not pursue the conversation any further. The present would just have to wait for the past.

TWO MOTHERS TOGETHER

I used my neighbour's phone to ring Mum and tell her about my surprise visitors. I cried as I tried to tell her. She was surprised but didn't sound shocked or even annoyed, and accepted the news quite well. I was relieved and happy after I had talked with her. I asked if I could bring Beatrice up after tea so they could meet each other. Mum agreed and I said it would only be a quick visit as we wouldn't stay long. As I walked back home I thought how wonderful she was to be so obliging. I wanted to share this day with her.

I waited anxiously for Ron to come home that afternoon. I was bursting with the news but managed to tell him casually that I'd had some visitors. He was a good listener and gradually got all the story out of me about my early morning visitors. He had such a gentle smile on his face and I knew he would have been wishing he was at home for that moment in history. He was pleased I had invited everyone back after tea so he could meet them and then have them follow us up to Beresfield.

We had two full carloads of people travelling in convoy to Mum's house. Jayne and Ken and the children didn't come so that made room for Uncle Cyril and Aunty Margaret, Beatrice and Kim. Our car was full with Ron, myself and our three boys.

We arrived shortly after seven o'clock. Mum and Neil greeted them all with a friendly smile and welcomed them inside. Mum never got used to entertaining people, I suppose because there were only the three of us in the house and we didn't have visitors.

Mum's house was small, and I felt embarrassed about having an extra nine people to fit into the little lounge room. Because of the size of the room, and the numerous conversations taking place at once, the two women didn't get much opportunity to speak to each other; plus I realised it was a very personal and private matter that should have happened on a less grand scale. The men were having a wonderful time conversing about cars, roads and travelling experiences. Beatrice and Kim sat together shyly, Mum sat next to Margaret and talked freely, while I made a cuppa in the kitchen.

It was like I was on the outside looking in as I watched my two mothers sitting in the same room together, and I hoped Mum wouldn't talk about me growing up, as it was such an emotional moment I didn't want to start crying. I just hoped they would like each other. Beatrice noticed Mum's little organ and asked her to sing a couple of songs. Mum sang a couple of gospel songs and we all joined in for 'Amazing Grace'. Beatrice tried to join in a couple of times and I could see from the corner of my eyes that she and Kim had the giggles; I thought it was a bit rude of them but I found out later that the key Mum sang in was way too high for Beatrice as she was an alto, and that's what was making them laugh.

After a cuppa and a singalong we took our visitors over to Tomago to visit Ron's parents. It was a ten-minute drive and as we drove there my heart was sinking. I was disappointed my two mothers hadn't communicated more, but Ron felt that there were too many other adults and children there who had obstructed their meeting.

SAME TOWN, SAME STARS

J ack and Betty were delighted to meet Beatrice. Ron's
sister Roslyn was there with her husband Bill, showing
her parents their new baby, Daniel. Roslyn was four years
younger than Ron and they were very close as brother and
sister. Ros was slim, organised, opinionated and very house
proud. I never felt good enough or up to her standard. Bill
had his own backhoe business and worked long hours; he
wasn't a talkative person, so he and I got on well. We often
bumped into them when visiting Ron's parents. I hadn't
seen the new baby yet so I spent the first fifteen minutes
discussing labour and post-natal issues with Ros, seemingly
forgetting about Beatrice and Kim. All the men had made
a direct detour to the shed, leaving Betty with us women
in the lounge room.

Betty wanted to speak to Beatrice but didn't know what
to say first. So, in all seriousness, she asked, 'Have you got

electricity in Coonamble yet?' Beatrice replied, 'Yeah, we got it on thirty years ago!' We all laughed. The more we thought about it the more we laughed. It broke the ice, and instantly everyone relaxed. Roslyn and Kim actually had tears rolling down their cheeks, then there was a second round as the others laughed at my funny, high-pitched squealing laughter, which brought all the men inside to see what was going on. Soon they joined in too. It created a relaxed atmosphere, and it seemed to melt all the tensions of the day.

Roslyn and Bill decided to leave as it was now 8.30 pm and their two older children, Paul, aged ten, and Fiona, aged nine, were very tired by this time. All the men went out to the front yard to see them off and Betty headed for the kitchen to put the kettle on for another cuppa. Roslyn waited in the kitchen with baby Daniel while Bill loaded the car and warmed up the motor. Betty was busy showing us all her electrical appliances that she had won in raffles at her club, and then she led Kim and Beatrice outside to the bird aviary to show off her birds by torchlight.

Roslyn and I sat in the kitchen and giggled about what had happened earlier. We could hear Beatrice and Kim giggling in the backyard as we heard them trip over things in the dark. They were out there wondering what we were laughing about inside, and when they came in again I could see Beatrice was a lot happier and relaxed. Kim talked Beatrice into singing a couple of songs while we enjoyed our cuppa.

Ron was talking to Bill in the driveway when they both heard her voice.

Bill asked, 'Who's that?'

'I don't know, it must be Beatrice,' Ron answered.

They both appeared in the kitchen doorway before she had finished the second verse. Bill was a stern person and it took a lot to move him to show his feelings, but when I looked up at Bill I saw that his eyes were filled with tears. I had goosebumps. The song Beatrice was singing was a beautiful gospel song that I had never heard before. It was called 'It is No Secret – What God Can Do'.

Beatrice's voice was strong, like one of those Negro spiritual singers I had seen on TV. It was an alto voice, and now I knew there was no way she could have sung in the same key as Mum, as she was a soprano. When she finished everyone clapped in amazement. Cyril brought in his guitar and backed her for a couple of numbers. She sang a few country and western songs. Some were Patsy Cline and Jim Reeves numbers. Ron's dad, Jack, kept saying, 'Isn't that a glorious voice?' We had no idea how much in demand this voice was out in the west.

Bill and Roslyn now decided to stay a bit longer and listen to Beatrice sing a few more songs. The women sat around the table and the men stood in the background enjoying the free concert. While I nursed Mark to sleep in my arms, I listened to the words of the next song, which was about a star that fell from heaven, and I had never heard that one either.

I took Kim into the spare room to give her a game of pool, thinking she wouldn't know how to play. As I took my shot I was trying to ignore the words of the next song Beatrice was singing, as I felt she was singing it to me. The words of this song were all about making up for past hurts. I didn't want to start crying. I had been holding back a flood of tears all day. All of Ron's family were into country music and they knew these songs but I didn't, as I had only grown up with gospel music. This was the first time I heard this song and it would be three years until I would hear it again. I found out then it was called 'Make the World Go Away', and sung by Jim Reeves.

Meanwhile back in the spare room I thought I was going to teach Kim how to play pool. I sank two balls and then she cleaned up the table. I felt a real dill. I found out that as there were no youth centres or cinemas in Coonamble, all the young people went to the pool hall to play pool seven days a week. Kim and I had a good laugh about it. She said, 'What do you think I do all day?' We were getting on very well.

Roslyn and Bill, who appreciated the importance of the visitors, stayed until we left. We had only ever played records together or listened to the Country Radio Show, which was on 2HD every Sunday night, when we went to visit Jack and Betty, so having an entertainer in our midst meant for quite a celebration. As we drove home that night I felt tickled pink. Ros and Bill had been so kind and Jack and Betty had been very hospitable, as always. I told Ron I was glad I met Beatrice now, and that I realised I had wasted a lot of time just being afraid of meeting her. Ron was saying, 'I love her voice. Isn't it fabulous?' I said, 'Mmmm,' agreeing with him as I had always done, but deep in my heart I still loved Mum's soprano voice, plus I felt obliged to remain loyal to her.

As we drove beside the Hunter River along the Hexham straight, I gazed at the moon's reflection on the mirror-like water. What a day in my life. Ron had anticipated this moment since the day he married me. I was so sorry that Dad had missed it. As I turned my head and checked out all my boys propped up against one another fast asleep, I realised they were too young to understand how special it was for me. I just hoped Mum would be able to sleep well, and not lie awake for hours thinking. This wasn't the time for regrets.

We travelled with the radio on, but Ron and I were silent, filled with our own thoughts. The stars shone so bright that night and here we were, in the same town, under the same stars, reunited again. I remembered how I once wished upon a falling star to meet my natural mother, and it seemed tonight my wish had been granted.

THE MISSING ONE

I didn't go to church the next day as I excitedly waited for my visitors to call in to say goodbye. It was a short visit, as they had a long trip ahead of them. Beatrice told us how very much she enjoyed meeting both our parents, and meeting Ron and her grandsons, and of course how good it was just to see me again. I said that it was lovely to meet them too, and my sisters. I gave my little niece and nephew a small magnetic game of draughts to help keep them occupied during the long trip back home.

As Kim and I walked up the driveway to my brother-in-law's car, I asked, 'What made you come out?'

She explained, 'Mum was missing you on Thursday because it was your birthday. She couldn't stop crying and Ken said, "Do you want to go to see Donna?" Mum said, "How am I gonna get to Newcastle?" and he said, "I'll take ya."'

Ron and I gave Beatrice and Kim a warm cuddle, and they gave us directions to take if ever we got to Coonamble. I watched the brown Falcon as it pulled away up over the hill and until it was out of sight. Ron and I happily walked arm in arm down the driveway and back inside. We lay down on the bed hugging one another, thinking about the past two days, just reliving all that had happened and all that was said. I cried for joy, and at the same time I was sad, wishing Dad could have been here for it all. Ron cried, as he knew it was the key piece that was missing from the emotional and psychological jigsaw of myself. Now I felt as if the sun shone through the cloud that had darkened my vision of my identity for over twenty years.

Even though Beatrice and I hadn't talked for hours on end, I had obtained enough information to fill in the missing gaps of my past. She told Ron and me that over a span of three months she had lost all seven of her children. There were the five eldest ones who were put on that welfare train, and the twins, three months old, who were only taken as far as Coonamble Hospital but who never went back home to the camp from there. So Beatrice never saw any of her children again.

It was so horribly awful for her waking up each morning and trying to live through a nightmare that kept manifesting itself throughout the daylight hours as well. She had wanted to kill herself so many times. She would have given up the will to live but her loving parents and sisters kept saying, 'They'll all come 'ome when they're ol' 'nough. You wait an see. You gotta be 'ere waitin for them. You know that ol' Murri spirit will come lookin for its own.' It was very hard trying to survive day by day. I can't put enough words on paper to express how her heart ached, but those who are mothers will understand without the words.

Beatrice gave birth to another four children in the succeeding years, two more boys and two girls: Les, Kim, Frank and Debbie. As each of her first seven children turned fifteen, they all found out and made their way back home on the same train tracks that had taken them away. I was the only one missing until now, thirteen years too late, as I was now twenty-eight. It felt good knowing I had seven brothers and three sisters, my dream of having lots of brothers and sisters had come true. My next dream was if only I could meet them all.

As Ron and I lay on the bed that morning, he asked, 'What are all their names and in which order do they come?' Each time I went through the list of names I was one short. Then the third time round Ron pointed out, 'You didn't count yourself.' We burst out laughing. So, in order, we were: Barry (Barry Butt), Michael (Widdy), Donna, Kevin (Sooty), Robert (Sly), Jayne and Wayne (twins), Les (Sonny), Kim (Tom), Frank (Darlie), and Debbie (the baby). It was a whole new concept for me to realise I was no longer an only child but that I was one of eleven. I felt kinda proud knowing I was the eldest girl too. I also thought it was nice how all the kids had nicknames.

Finally, the headache I had been wearing all day from all the excitement multiplied into a migraine. Ron left me alone to sleep it off. When I woke I thought that it had really all been a dream.

The Promise

DESTINATION COONAMBLE

Beatrice had invited us to Coonamble for Christmas, which was only four weeks away, but I knew we couldn't afford such a trip. But on 27 December 1981 we left Newcastle, destination Coonamble. Ron had been saving a little bit each week all year long for Christmas holidays, and totally surprised me when he told me he could take me home to Coonamble after Christmas Day if I wanted. This was my Christmas present and I really looked forward to a trip away. At times I felt locked in the house, and housewives need a holiday just as anybody else who is working. I was also pleased for Darren's sake, so that he too could have some news about where he spent his Christmas holidays.

It was a very hot day to travel but the heat was not going to interfere with the excitement of the trip and the adventure ahead. After travelling for a few hours we noticed the change in the outline of the land. On the other side of the mountain range the land became flatter with each kilometre. Along the edge of the bitumen I could see the bright red soil that was underneath the tar, and in a strange way I fell in love with it. It was comforting to watch it track along the side of the road. I could breathe in its warmth. It was very welcoming – I could quite easily become mesmerised watching it.

Every now and then when we criss-crossed the railway track it drew my attention to the real purpose of the trip. Kilometre after kilometre as we followed the train line, it brought back a flood of memories of my first train ride, and I recalled that endless noise of the clicketty-clack along the track. Each time we crossed over the tracks it made me feel more nervous. Each time it drew my attention to the real purpose of the trip. Doubts began to swamp my heart. If I had been driving the car alone, I would have turned around and headed back to Newcastle. I'm not sure what I was afraid of, but something was confronting my spirit. I wondered if Ron felt as uncertain as I did, but when I glanced at him I could see he was happy and smiling as he drove in the heat of the day. He had wanted to take me home ever since we got married, but I had never imagined it would actually happen.

I thought I better prepare Ron for what lay in store, so I finally said, 'You know they're all going to be very dark.' Half a question and half a statement.

He laughed and replied, 'Yes, I know'.

I couldn't tell him I was scared, so I said, 'Aren't you scared?'

He answered, 'No. If I was I wouldn't have married you.'

I always took my fears to the Lord in prayer, so as the

journey progressed I silently prayed and asked for wisdom and strength to accept whatever I would be confronted with. I asked the Lord to bless Mum while I was away and to make sure she wasn't lonely or felt forgotten while I went back home to the land of my birth.

When Mum had remarried six years previously she remained in her house at Beresfield. Kel Chandler was a quiet-natured man and Mum loved having company each day and someone to care for. Caring for Kel filled in the hours for Mum and I was glad that she had someone to care for her as I did what Dad always wanted me to do, and that was, when the time was right, to meet my people. Kel preferred to be called Neil so our boys called him Poppy Neil. When I first met Neil, he told me he grew up with a couple of Aboriginal boys and that they were real good mates. Neil was familiar with many Aboriginal boxers as he'd been a boxer himself in his youth. Boxing was a popular sport in the fifties and he'd met many boxers. Neil had met Bea and Uncle Cyril and knew how important the trip was going to be; he reassured me he would look after Mum, and told me to enjoy myself.

We expected the road out west to be old, rugged, and full of potholes, but we were cruising at 120 kilometres an hour on what, compared to the city roads, was equal to a highway. I wished I had my own brake pedal so that I could slow the car down until I stopped feeling nervous. According to directions, we only had two hours' drive ahead of us. Ron was talking on the CB radio to a station in South Australia, which helped take my mind off things for a while. I kept an eye on the signposts that flashed by. When we zoomed by one that had 'Coonamble 10k', I said, 'I'd better do my hair and put my face on.'

Ron laughed: 'At this speed we'll be there in three minutes!'

'Well, slow down!' I yelled.

We pulled into Coonamble, amazed with the wide streets and finding the town to be much bigger than we anticipated. There were plenty of shops, a TAB, motels, parks, sports ovals, churches, a caravan park, video parlours and taxis. In fact, it looked pretty much the same as Cardiff. With one exception. The majority of people on the streets were Aboriginal. It seemed like every dark eye was upon us. They knew we were strangers as they watched our aqua Torana cruise down the main drag.

I was happy to be in town but glad Ron was with me to help deal with my fears. When we arrived, my fears just vanished. I think if I had seen a train or train station right then, I would have turned limp and cried my heart out, but instead, as we drove over the Coonamble Bridge, I looked down at the Castlereagh River flowing below, my eyes filled with tears, and I thought, 'Yes, I'm home.'

CELEBRITIES

We arrived in Coonamble at 6.30 pm and even though Ron didn't know which side of town to go to, he drove instinctively in the general direction and came upon the right place – Broad Street, number three. It was a small fibro house owned by the Housing Commission, painted a pale bluey-grey colour, and with a lovely little garden. We surprised everyone by our late arrival. They had expected us to be home in time for Christmas Day and thought after Boxing Day that we weren't coming at all.

It had been such a hot day to travel out west that, when we arrived, I headed straight to the kitchen and filled a glass with water. I guzzled down a glass and didn't realise that it was bore water until I emptied the glass. It was a horrible taste. We soon learned that you had to boil the water first and let it cool. My two younger brothers, who had been sitting on the lounge, watched me grab the drink and they laughed as I pulled a disgusted look at my first taste of bore water. I had heard about Darlie and Sonny from Bea's letters and at last I met them. Sonny was slim, tall, dark and handsome, plus he had the whitest smile I ever saw on a young man. He was a man of few words. He smiled a lot and if he did speak it was in almost a whisper. Darlie was the youngest son. He had straight hair and his features and hairstyle reminded me of the American Indians.

It was too hot to sit inside so we all sat out under the tree in the front yard. In all honesty, the only time I'd ever done that was on a picnic. As I sat there being polite, I remember thinking, I hope the neighbours aren't watching. I listened to my brothers' accents and loved it: they had the same twang as Aunty Margaret. As I was raised in the city, I spoke just like everyone else, there was no hint of accent in my voice. It was ten degrees cooler under the tree as we sat there relaxing after the long hard drive. We watched the most lustrous sunset. Sunsets were always one of my favourite things, and I drank in the glorious orangey-red sky that promised another heatwave tomorrow. Time took on a whole new meaning here, for instance, no-one worried about tea until after sunset, when the house cooled down a bit.

At the end of the hallway Sonny sat in his bedroom playing his guitar. He played the same song, his favourite piece, over and over trying to perfect it. The song was 'Apache' by The Shadows, and ever since then, each time I hear that song, it reminds me of my first trip back home. It became evident that music was a significant quality in the Welsh blood line, it was something that enabled the Aboriginal spirit to live on.

During the next couple of days there was plenty of

coming and going. The brothers, sisters, aunties and cousins all dropping in to meet us. This was the first time I saw people sleep on lounges, and on a bare floor. As long as there was floor space you could always put people up. This was a real education for me. Everyone in town was so friendly. I even met the old lady who had driven us to the railway station about twenty-three years ago.

Bea explained who all the people were in the family photo albums, and told me the history of these people. As I studied the photographs on the wall I tried to remember all their names. I was drawn to a magnificent-looking man who had a stern look, masculine cheekbones, lips that would melt a woman, strong dark eyes, and who wore his hat tipped in a dignified manner. He was the most dignified man I'd ever seen, with the strongest Aboriginal features. I was captivated. I secretly wished he was my father.

'Who is he?' I asked my heart. Beatrice sat in the kitchen watching me. I finally and wishfully asked, 'Who is in the large photo next to our wedding photo?'

She told me, 'That's your grandfather, Jimmy Welsh from Pilliga Scrub.'

I said to myself, 'You're gorgeous. I wish I knew you.'

Beatrice continued, 'He lived with us at the old camp. He loved music. He could play the spoons and button accordion, and he could make a violin talk. He had a wonderful sense of humour and all the black and white fellas respected him. He was there the day they took you away. He kept sayin, "We gotta find them kids and bring them home." He died long time ago. Granny went a bit silly in her mind in her last couple of months but before she died she asked, "Has Donna come home yet?"'

It made me feel embarrassed to realise that they were all

thinking about me but I didn't want to think about them. All my relations were very dark and this was the first time I was actually mixing in with them. All day long and for half of the night relations and family friends stopped by to meet the lost daughter and her family from Newcastle. We went down the street the next day and I was shocked to see about fifty of my relations standing on the corner waiting for us. It took ages to get introduced. They nearly all looked the same as me. I greeted everyone with a kiss on the cheek. At least fifteen minutes later, I was introduced to an elderly Aboriginal man. As I walked towards him, Tom and Beatrice stood laughing and waving their hands to stop me, saying, 'No, no, he's not one of ours.' He was coming back for another kiss. 'You all look the same to me,' I said.

They were friendly people, accepting us so well. I got the impression they had all expected us to return one day. It was strange being the talk of the town. Every shop we went to, people would be talking about us. Even the man at the takeaway shop said, 'You must be the sister from Newcastle.' Darren, who was ten, said, 'Mum, have you noticed how they think we must be important or something?' Ron and I did feel like celebrities.

All those years the Lord was working on my insecurities, teaching me humility, identity, acceptance — and how to love people and not their possessions, how to love unconditionally. He had prepared me for this time. Now I noticed the simple lives the people lived. The old bits and pieces of furniture, the photos that were their most treasured possessions. Nearly every house had at least one dog. Ron and the boys liked dogs but I didn't, I couldn't even pat them without having to wash my hands immediately afterwards, and I couldn't get over how they walked freely in and out of the houses. I accepted the people and their lifestyle with the obvious different values, but I knew I didn't want to live here. It was deeper than mere pride: I knew my values were different, I didn't feel like I belonged. My position as a friendly onlooker was what separated me and yet there was a real, painful guilt in that separation. How long would it take until I felt like I belonged? The harder, secret question was, Did I want to belong? I was more comfortable in my world where things were in their place, where there was a certain time to do certain things, a sophisticated order and expectations to adhere to. And yet despite all of that expectation, within me flowed a rebellious river, a wanting to escape, to inhale freedom. But I was too conditioned, too cowardly, to leave the ordered, normal life.

AUNTY TAM

The next day, at about 4.30 in the afternoon, a white Valiant pulled up at the front of the house. The four people sitting in the lounge room all left silently, as if on cue.

Kim said to Bea, 'She's here.'

'Who?' I asked.

'Aunty Tam,' they replied. Just one more aunt, I thought.

She entered the room. A small-framed woman with dark eyes and skin like Grandfather's. She walked across the room slowly.

'Donna Maria,' she said in a soft, kind voice as I stood to meet her.

We stood there, eye to eye, hand in hand, arms outstretched. Although her eyes never left mine, I knew she was completely checking me out. She smiled lovingly, then I kissed her. When she let go of my hands, I paused and waited for her to move. When she sat, I sat also. Aunty Tam sat next to me on the lounge. Ron was in one arm-chair across the small lounge room and Beatrice rested in the other. I introduced Ron and the boys. She nodded with approval, but all she could say was, 'I don't believe it.' I fixed my eyes on a spot on the carpet square. Beatrice sat watching us. Everyone sat in silence. Ron lit a cigarette to fill in time. I couldn't think of a thing to say. Beatrice and Aunty Tam communicated with their eyes but didn't speak out loud. Still no-one spoke, no car drove past, no dog barked. We all sighed one after another.

Finally, Ron said, 'Well, if someone doesn't speak you'll all cry and from where I'm sitting I'll get drenched. I'll have a shower later.'

We all laughed. It was just like someone had pressed pause and then released the button. Aunt told us where she lived and said we should call around tomorrow. Then Beatrice told us how close she and her sister Tam were, even as kids, how they did everything together. Now that both their parents had passed away, they always went to each other when they had a problem. These two sisters were like the welfare workers in the family. Everyone came to them for advice and they did their best trying to get food, financial assistance for emergencies or just generally supporting anyone going through stress or a crisis.

On our last day we went to Aunty Tam's house. It was an old shack of a house with most of her treasures coming from the tip, like Ron's Aunty Lorna. Her husband, Uncle Bill, was in the backyard repairing the motor on a beige Ford, and when he heard another motor running he pulled his head out to investigate. When he saw us, he dropped everything and ran to meet us, calling out, 'Tam, look who's here.' He kissed me all over, crying and saying over and over, 'My baby's back, my baby's come home.' Then he cuddled and kissed me and started all over again: 'It's my baby, my baby's back.'

I was rather confused and embarrassed. He was a big man and he hugged me tightly. He smelled of beer and I could smell beer all over my face where he had kissed me. It was the first time anyone had ever kissed me with alcohol on their breath. Then Uncle shook hands firmly with Ron, wearing the biggest smile. As some young children came from the house, Uncle said again, 'This is my baby, this is my baby.'

I still didn't know what he meant. He was delighted to meet Ron and admired the boys. His smile never disappeared. Uncle showed us into the house where Aunty Tam sat at the table, her eyes wet with tears. She was quiet, and I didn't know if she was shy, nervous, or too emotional to speak. Uncle asked Ron what type of work he was in. He asked the names of our sons. We stayed about fifteen minutes then we had to go and pack.

Back at home I said to Beatrice, 'I don't know why, but out of all the aunties, I like Aunty Tam the best. She's quiet, I don't know why but I just like her the most.'

Then Beatrice told me that Aunty Tam had lost her baby when Beatrice was five months pregnant with me, and Beatrice had said, 'You name this baby, she'll make up for the little one you lost.' She named me Donna Maria, so in a way I really was *their* baby girl.

MY TREE

By now I had met most of my brothers and sisters, however Butt (Barry) was living in Queensland, and Sooty (Kevin) and Widdy (Michael) were away so I hadn't met them; Wayne had come home once but never returned so I couldn't meet him either.

Robby was tall, very dark and very thin. He lived on the other side of town. I didn't see much of him, but I remember I always thought that Aboriginal people had wide flat noses whereas he had a very long straight nose, like one of the actors on *Roots*, an American series on TV at the time; so I learned that the popular perception about the Aboriginal race having broad noses was a stereotype perpetuated by the media.

Robby was at home the day my first letter arrived, and as Bea was staying with friends in Walgett, he took the letter across because he knew it would thrill Bea to know where

I was. Walgett was an hour's drive north and so Robby set out trying to hitchhike up there. It was one of those days when he couldn't get a lift and he virtually walked half the way over. He felt real proud that he was the one who was at home and first knew of my letter, and that he was the one who passed it on to Bea.

I had only met a couple of branches from my family tree and knew it would take a long time to fill in all the blanks. Kim appeared to have an important role in the family as she took care of all the nieces and nephews. Debbie was the youngest girl and repeatedly brought kids home who were in need of a feed. I didn't push myself on any of them as I knew we all had to get to know each other first. I met Aunty Joan who lived in Coonamble and Aunty Audrey who lived in Walgett and who had made a special trip across to meet Ron, myself and our sons. I knew these two aunts had rhythm and loved music. All of the aunts were musical and sang beautifully together, but these two lived and breathed music and danced their way through life.

It suddenly occurred to me to ask, 'Where did we used to live?'

Beatrice said, 'Follow me.' She led me down her back-yard to the adjoining block. We looked over the fence and Bea motioned with her head. 'This was our camp. This was where we all lived with the old fella,' meaning Grandfather. 'See that tree.' My eyes followed where she pointed, and I could see a huge tree that would have been close to forty feet high. 'You used to climb that. Grandfather worked for a family and they let us set up camp on his property. Real good white people.'

My first thoughts were: This was the scrawny little tree I used to climb. I swallowed hard and tears formed in my eyes as I stood looking up at the tree. I remembered a group of carefree children sitting in its cool shade talking, and the uncles sitting under it smoking and sharing funny work stories. I remembered how I loved dressing it up as a Christmas tree. Beatrice had quietly slipped away as if she knew I was revisiting my childhood. I stood alone now beside the majestic gum tree, remembering echoes from the past, the people, their voices and their singing. I remembered the day we came home and first saw the gramophone. So many songs had been sung since then.

The tree was as important as a lounge room. It was the centre of the camp. This was where people would sit for hours on end either carving eggs, singing or simply watching life. This was our TV. This was how we learned our roles, watching adults' behaviour, and there was always plenty to laugh about. The memories made me feel sad. To be here one day, gone the next and then to come back a stranger. I was still lost. Lost in my new life and lost in the old one.

How unbelievable it all was. That this particular land where the family lived thirty years ago should be subdivided, and the tree left untouched. That the Housing Commission should build houses on this land. I wondered how Beatrice must have felt when she realised the house the Department gave her was on the very same ground as the old family camp. This tree had survived zoning, development and fire and yet it stood equal to the other surrounding trees. It had grown tall and its roots were strong and steadfast.

This was the land where her babies took their first steps, learned how to swim and climb trees. Now each one of her children had returned to the land of their birth. This belonged to me or I belonged to it. The pain of the day I

was taken away came flooding back. I cried the day I was
sent away and I was crying now because I was back. As I
wiped the tears, in the distance I could hear the call of the
currawongs. They're still here. Some things returned while
other things never ever left.

COMING HOME

The river had changed. There wasn't any water flowing. Just a dried-up river bed. The boys couldn't get over how people walked across it as a short cut into the main street to do their shopping and then walked back over it with arms full of plastic shopping bags filled with groceries. Darren said, 'Just like Moses and the Red Sea.'

The town's water supply was pumped daily as there was water thirty feet under the river bed. None of us liked the taste of the bore water, including the locals. It smelled as bad as it tasted. Although the days and nights were hot, we endured the very different dry heat. Unlike the coastal heat out west there was little humidity. We saw some glorious orangey-red sunsets across miles of paddocks where the only buildings in sight were the silhouettes of the wheat silos.

Time stood still. You didn't have to be on time for anything. You didn't have your meal according to the clock. It was a more relaxed pace of life. The boys loved the freedom and played well with their cousins. They were preoccupied with running their Matchbox toys through the red dirt or talking to the galahs. Kids were always coming and going. There was a slippery dip and swing set in the block adjacent to the backyard and there were plenty of playmates. Darren and Tim enjoyed all the new things to do and see. Someone had a horse and brought it over every day and gave the children rides. Then one of the uncles brought his horse around and gave the children rides all afternoon. It was the first time my boys had sat on a horse. When they returned from the pony ride they found my sister Kim feeding the other children ice-cream straight from the ice-cream container. There was only one large spoon and the children seemed content with having one spoonful of ice-cream at a time. My boys had always had their own individual plates and spoons, but they joined in as they loved ice-cream too.

On the morning we planned to leave, Beatrice and Kim invited me to go shopping with them. I was surprised to learn the reason for us women to go alone across the bridge and down the main street. At the paper shop they purchased two little souvenirs. Kim gave me a miniature cup and saucer with the Lord's Prayer printed on the plate and Beatrice bought me a tea towel with the words 'Greetings from Coonamble' written in bold print across the top. How I treasured these first gifts from my sister and my mother.

It had been an enjoyable visit. Meeting so many friendly people. Seeing their way of life. Listening to their accents and listening to them sing and cry. Meeting cousins and aunties, my relations, but more than that, knowing they accepted us and loved us. I had gained so many answers to questions that I had kept filed for decades. I was really glad for Ron that my sisters had married non-Aboriginal men so he didn't feel left out. It was like joining pieces of a jigsaw puzzle, only I didn't know what picture I was building. The pieces were coming together but there were still critical pieces missing.

As we drove down the little side streets, we were fare-welled by many dark smiling faces, adults and children waving to us. Dark people waving as we drove across the Coonamble Bridge, and whistles and waves as we drove past the post office for the last time. It had been an adventure. Ron and I had much to discuss as we headed for our home in Newcastle. Darren and Tim also shared their favourite things about the trip. Ron and I compared notes as to what we had expected and how we felt now after exposing our-selves to the family.

I had expected to see a lot of drunks hanging around but I only saw two the whole time. This is what the media always portrays and this was one of the reasons why I was concerned about being confronted with a lifestyle that was so opposite to the values that Ron and I had. But now I had my own opinion about Aboriginal people and it wasn't the view presented by the media. These people showed Ron and me the utmost courtesy. Sharing every-thing. Talking freely. Never swearing. Teaching me about our family tree. And Ron never felt offended because of the colour of his skin.

My greatest realisation was that Beatrice was just a normal person. She didn't fit any of the images I had built up of her. She was honest, sincere, and loved by everyone. She would help anyone who came to her doorstep for help. She was the Mum Shirl of Coonamble. Everyone called her 'Aunty Beat'; her humble dwelling, the little grey fibro Housing Commission place, was a refuge for young and old alike. No fancy bed, just a pillow on the lino floor, a blanket or two. It was shelter, where people could be sung to sleep by her tender voice and warmed by her love. Here one found a few hours' peace from the storms of life.

She vowed she would never send anyone from her doorstep ever since that shattering day in 1960 when the government took her seven children away. No words can express her anguished memories, the anger, the stinging of a broken heart which took twenty-three years to heal. Twenty-three long, miserable, lonely, destructive years waiting for her children to return to her arms. But they did. One by one, just as Grandfather said they would. They came home and found her arms outstretched like a big hen giving protection to her little chicks. She felt needed but more than that, she was now giving her love to the original seven who had been denied her love because of ruthless government policies.

As we travelled hour after hour, I found I had so many happy memories that would keep me going. All the lovely faces and the sound of laughter again. There were so many highlights of the trip, the town and the people who lived in it. What a time it had been, and the time had been right. Some of the chains I had dragged around with me all my life now fell off and I had a sense of being free, but I also knew that in some ways I was still a prisoner.

28 April, 1973 – Ron Meehan and me: love doesn't have a colour. Three years earlier, when Ron didn't even know my name, he'd told his mates: 'I'm going to marry that girl.'

Left: Jimmy Welsh, my maternal grandfather, who would sing me to sleep with his favourite song, 'Beautiful Dreamer'.

Below: My new mum and dad were very loving towards me. Me at the age of eight, with my parents, Elizabeth and Tim Popov.

Four of my eight brothers (*from left to right*): Frank (always called Darlie), Michael (Widdy), Barry and Robby. In 1975, when this photograph was taken, my brothers believed we would never all be together again.

My brother Les (Sonny) and his partner, Penny, with my sister Kim (Tom), in 1994.

My husband, Ron, in 1991.

From left to right: Aunty Audrey, Aunty Joan and Aunty Tam singing together at the Beatrice Welsh Memorial Day in 1995. My mother and her sister Tam were very close.

'If only the folks back home could see us now.' *From left to right:* Aunty Tam, me, Widdy's wife Rita, Aunty Ivy and my brother Widdy at the Sydney Town Hall in 1998 for the Sydney Writers' Festival.

My special tree, which I climbed every day as a child.
When I stood beneath it twenty-two years later,
I remembered echoes from the past. This tree had been the
centre of the camp, it was where we played and sang and
listened to stories.

My youngest son, Mark, in 1991.

My eldest son, Darren, going off to America to work as a pit crew member for the American Racing Team, in 1993.

From left to right: My youngest son, Mark; me; my second son, Tim, and his girlfriend, Sherriden; my eldest son, Darren, and his partner, Lindy, in 1999.

Beatrice Welsh, my mum, in 1984.

Hello, Brother

Four months after my coming home trip, I received a letter from Beatrice proudly announcing she had become a Christian and saying how she loved church. She especially loved singing the beautiful old hymns. I could tell by her letter that she was real excited. She wrote, 'I never been so happy. I born again.' The letter arrived on 6 April 1982, four years to the very day that I had gone to that meeting in Toronto and met Aunty Margaret and learned the address where my natural mother was living. Both Bea and I were different people now and more at peace with ourselves and with each other. No longer strangers.

About twice a year, Uncle Cyril would drop in for a quick visit to see how we all were. He kept in close contact with his Aunty Beatie so he knew everything even before he asked how things were going between us. One day I received an invitation for us to attend his daughter's wedding, which was to be held at Cardiff in the Church of Christ. I was surprised that we received an invitation as I hadn't met Cyril's eldest daughter Meranda yet, but I was also excited at the prospect of having a social night out. Our boys were our world and we never left them, we never went out, except to Ron's parents' house when we were invited for tea.

I lay-byed a lovely soft pink dress. I could only afford a new dress for special occasions and so I looked forward to getting dressed up. Bea had been asked to sing so Ron and I assumed she would stay with us for a few days and we anticipated her visit. Beatrice wrote and told me that Sooty and Aunty Ivy would be there from Walgett and to keep my eye out for them. I hadn't met either of them, yet I looked forward to it. I knew Aunty Ivy was a great Christian and worked lovingly amongst her people in Walgett. I was extremely keen to meet her. Then Bea notified us that she was not well enough to travel and she asked Ron and me to represent her at the wedding. I was very disappointed but felt obliged to go even though I didn't think I would know anyone.

This was the first Aboriginal wedding I had ever been to and I wasn't sure what to expect. I felt really nervous walking into the church, as so many eyes were staring at us. It was a large wedding and the church was full. Ron and I stood at the doorway looking for seats and trying to ignore the stares from all the dark faces. I noticed a tall, well-dressed young Aboriginal man striding over to where Ron and I stood. Walking behind him was an elderly woman who looked like Bea and I thought they had to be sisters. The dark stranger stretched out his arms and shook hands with Ron and greeted him saying, 'Hello, brother.'

Ron shook hands keenly and said, 'You must be Sooty, and this must be Aunty Ivy.'

Sooty then kissed me and said in a deep husky voice, 'Hello, sis.'

The last time I'd seen him he was two years old and now he was a debonair young man who carried that same dignity of Grandfather. He introduced us to Aunty Ivy and led us back to their seats. She looked so much like Beatrice.

I admired all the lovely Aboriginal people. I was fascinated by how refined they all looked dressed up. Aunty Margaret looked gracefully elegant as she patiently waited for her daughter Meranda and Uncle Cyril to appear. Other than myself I had never seen another Aboriginal bride. Meranda was the most beautiful bride I ever saw in her white dress that contrasted against her brown velvet skin. While Meranda and Bob signed their papers Uncle Cyril sang with his guitar. As I listened to him singing I suddenly remembered Beatrice and I thought that she should be on the stage singing.

I started crying, at first for Mum not being there, then because it was the first time I met Sooty and how kind he was to Ron, making him feel welcome, and then because I thought Aunty Ivy was so beautiful. I was also feeling guilty because I wasn't as free with Sooty as they were with him. In some way there was still a barrier between us.

The church women all contributed towards the wedding feast and for the first time I saw damper. We left the reception about 9.30, as I wasn't used to being away from my boys. I ended up bringing home the most absolutely gorgeous dark brown baby girl. My cousin Doll-Doll and a group of Aboriginal people from Sydney, Walgett, Coonamble and Lightning Ridge all wanted to go to the Cardiff

Workers Club after the reception and as that wasn't our scene I jumped at the opportunity to look after Robyn. Little Robyn was three months old, all dressed up in a fancy pink pinch-pleated dress. She was a picture. I couldn't take my eyes off her. Ron was bewitched by her also. We had never seen a dark baby before.

We had baby Robyn for the night, and she was so contented it didn't bother her being left with total strangers. The boys were also intrigued with her and there was a constant stream of observers peering over the cot admiring the little doll-like visitor. How I wished I could keep this little bundle of joy. Ron and I were in complete awe of her. How I wished she was mine. I wondered, If I had a baby girl, would she look like Robyn? I also felt so privileged that Doll-Doll had entrusted me with her pride and joy, as I was a stranger.

I took little Robyn and showed her off to my next-door neighbours, the two women who ran the corner shop, and proudly showed her off to a lovely family a few streets away who Ron knew from working with them at the dockyards. Everyone had a genuine admiration for this gorgeous little black doll. I knew these people were sincere but I couldn't help but wonder whether everyone in society would call her beautiful. Why is it that people can accept a coloured baby but find it difficult to accept a teenager? If they accepted her now, would they still feel the same way in another ten years?

UNCLE HUBERT DOOLAN

T hings were slowly coming together for me. Being a mum and having more experience with my children. Running a household. Meeting more women from Tim's preschool and coming to terms with my Aboriginal family. I always found it difficult being the only Aboriginal person wherever I was, but the non-Aboriginal women at church encouraged me and reinforced positive messages about me and my children. The women's group would meet at each other's place once a month and I formed friendships with women from all ages, women who were sincere and made me feel part of their group. All of us shared children's clothes, books and conversations about nearly everything from cooking, shopping, running a house, effective parenting and being a good wife. I gained skills that equipped me for around the house and so I started feeling more secure about who I was and the type of person I wanted to be. It goes without saying I enjoyed being with such lovely women and found it was quality time well spent.

This was an important learning time for me about the world of people, within this gentle and caring sub-group in society. I needed to meet people who showed me I was accepted and loved, so this was really healing time for my mind and heart. In conjunction with that it was also important learning time in my walk of faith, as I started to hand over problems and just got on with life instead of procrastinating or being filled with anger.

As I listened to the other women sharing their problems and learned how they worked through them, in time I taught myself to work through my problems; when there was no immediate solution I knew how to hand over big problems to the Lord and allow Him to deal with them. This freed me from anger, worry and fear and enabled me to become a new person filled with joy, love and hope.

When June McMurray, our minister Don's wife, had first approached me to teach the preschool class at Sunday School and take a weekly scripture class at Hillsborough Primary School, I had declined as I felt I wasn't smart enough. But I'd found it was valuable time as I was comfortable working with children the same age as my own kids, and speaking to a class gave me the confidence I needed to communicate.

There were many other factors which had contributed to my gaining confidence. Apart from the influence from my church family, teaching Sunday School and taking the scripture class, Ron's interest was CB radio and so we also had a CB family. We made lots of contacts with people from all over Australia. Hiding behind a microphone helped me to gain so much confidence and build my communication skills, plus I had a real hunger for knowledge. I still used the local library and lost myself in books.

One Friday night a stranger knocked at our front door. He was extremely dark and had vivid white hair. He told us he was Uncle Hubert from Coonamble, and asked if he could have a bed for the night. On rare occasions, we'd only ever had children sleep over, so having an adult, a relation, sleep the night made it extra special. Uncle Hubert was a storyteller who enjoyed entertaining us for hours. He told us about all the funny memories he had of my brothers and aunties. He wasn't a singer but he loved spinning a yarn and telling his jokes. Ron and I had tears running down our faces from so much laughter, he was so amusing. His eyes danced as he told his yarns, sitting comfortably on the floor, using his hands for extra emphasis. He was pure theatre, and knew he had a captive audience. The boys were completely taken by this man. We found out that Uncle Hubert wasn't as old as we originally thought as in his early twenties his hair apparently went white overnight. He was a delight and I was glad that we were related somehow.

My favourite story was about the Coonamble Show. Each year it would rain at showtime, so the council asked if he could come and do an Aboriginal rain dance, in order to keep the rain away that week. They paid him $50 up front. He got dressed up in a laplap, painted himself up, danced and chanted a song in lingo. He looked the part and took the cash, only problem was it was the first time he ever put on a laplap, and the only song he knew was a song Grandfather used to sing from Pilliga. He sang in lingo so the white people had no clue what he was singing but the Aboriginal people knew he was singing, 'He sends the rainbow, the lovely rainbow, he sends the rainbow with the rain', and it rained for three days and three nights.

Uncle Hubert retold the story of how he idolised Beatrice and thought the world of her. He went to church meetings with her as he loved to hear her sing. In 1983, Beatrice gave her first testimony at a church rally in Gilgandra, speaking about how she had found her daughter twenty-three years after being separated and thanking God for bringing us back together. Uncle Hubert was with her that day. He wore an old second-hand suit from the op shop and glowed with pride as he entered the old church building. He took along his old-fashioned tape recorder and recorded the meeting. The spoken words were not very audible but he knew that even from where he sat the recorder would have no problem picking up the voice of Beatrice Welsh. Now he handed me the cassette with so much pride that his face beamed with joy. We had no idea how valuable this tape would become.

Ron and I played the precious tape over and over, amazed at the power of the recording. A few days later, I played the tape for Mum at Bero (Beresfield). After she heard it, we both sat at the dining table and prayed. We had tears of joy. Mum gave thanks to God, and said, 'This is a marvellous story. It's wonderful how things have all turned out.'

We never saw our funny man again. He died six months later. Now we knew he was on a mission. Now we understood the urgency of his visit. I often wonder if he knew he was going to die soon. People in Coonamble can't remember when he died but come showtime, there's a smile that crosses many a face as they recall Uncle Hubert, the Rain Dancer.

THE PROMISE

I shared photos, letters and all my experiences with my mum from Newcastle. We were both learning about my Aboriginal family. We both firmly believed God had arranged our reunion and so acceptance was much easier. Mum and I had a unique love which strengthened with each year. She loved her family as we were all she had in Australia. Ron was the best son-in-law.

During 1983 Aunty Tam's husband Uncle Bill died suddenly. We didn't have enough money to go back for the funeral but we saved enough to make it back home for Tom's (Kim's) twenty-first in 1984.

We spent five days in Coonamble during this visit. We took the rain with us and it was a welcome sight as there hadn't been any rain for over a year. It had been a heatwave the day before we headed due west. The boys were three years older and enjoyed travelling a bit more than the first trip out. We kept the Esky filled with ice water from home as we had learned what a thirsty trip the dry heat made.

Travelling on the road out west again we noticed the upgraded bridges and road work along the way. The road from the city to the bush had marked improvements. There was a twelve-kilometre gravel road just after Mendooran but even this had been recently covered with bitupave.

The boys took notice of the brightly coloured birds they saw feeding beside the roadway. Tim had pestered us for three years to catch a baby galah so he could teach it to talk. Galahs lined the roadside pecking at seeds which flew out of trucks carrying grain. Tim was the middle child and wanted a pet to keep him company. He loved animals. The bush budgies and rosellas out west had vivid colours not to be compared to the ones we saw in the city.

Darren had a love of trucks and the trip passed quickly for him as he kept his eyes out for the oncoming vehicles. Ron talked on CB radio to interstate stations carried by skip, and I had taught myself to crochet which kept me occupied. Driving to Coonamble the second time was much more relaxing than the first trip. Beatrice's house looked the same but I was a more mature, casual and accepting person.

Tom's twenty-first was a family barbeque in the backyard. Close to a hundred relations were coming. Barry came around early in the morning to meet Ron and myself. He was so dark and shiny, and he was extra friendly, not shy like most of the brothers. He joked with Ron and I was amazed how they all called him Brother. Barry didn't stay long as he had just got in from Queensland and was bursting to catch up with all his mates. He returned later to show off his new baby girl. As I held the tiny beautiful doll I fell in love with her as I had with baby Robyn. My eyes filled with tears as I never knew children could look so beautiful.

I asked, 'What's her name?'

'Belinda,' said Barry.

Right then I got goosebumps. I received my first brand-new doll on my ninth birthday. I named her Belinda and I chose that name during all my pregnancies if the baby happened to be a girl. The same eerie feeling came over me when I went to Tom's new flat. She had the same ornaments in her house as I did. She had the autumn tonings like I did and there on her wall hung an autumn painting that I had picked out for my lounge room but had never had the money to buy. Tom and I laughed the same and Ron found it difficult to distinguish which was which.

Ron was asked to duck down to the train station to pick up Sooty who was coming from Sydney. Distance was nothing to people out west, as Ron later learned the train station was in Dubbo, two hours' drive each way. While he was gone, all the women were busy preparing salads and cooking cakes.

As it was a special occasion, there were relations in town from all over the state. I met Widdy but it wasn't as emotional as meeting Barry. Widdy had fairer skin than I did and lovely green eyes. He was very reserved. The only brother missing was Wayne. Apparently he had come home when he was seventeen but couldn't handle the culture shock. How I wished I could reach out to him as I knew how he must have felt, but I also realised how far I had come out of my shell since I first came home. I was slowly working through my identity crisis.

The party was very informal. Everyone came who was expected. I was surprised that Tom got hardly any gifts, but realised the main essence was the family reunion, the food, drink, and singalong. When everybody was fed, we all sat in a circle in the backyard. There was a small fire going and people were really enjoying themselves. Beatrice began to play her piano accordion and sang everyone's request. The singing went on for hours. At 10.30 I hadn't seen Ron for over half an hour and wondered where he'd got to. All I could see were silhouettes around the fire and none resembled his profile, so I thought he was inside the house.

As I was walking down the path I met Barry. After saying how good it was to see me again and what a good man Ron was, he put his heavy hand on my shoulder and said, 'I want you to promise me one thing. Will you promise me?'

'If I can,' I replied, as I thought he was going to ask for money.

'No. No. I want you to promise me one thing, sister.'

I chuckled. 'If I can,' I replied suspiciously.

He said, 'Promise me! You'll write a book about this. You're the smartest out of all of us. Promise me.'

My eyes filled with tears. 'Yes, I will,' I promised.

I had been daydreaming about the idea for over a year but didn't think I was smart enough. This was like confirmation and I gained confidence from the fact that someone else had confidence in me. This was a sign. A sign to convince me, to help me to start believing in myself. It is so very hard when you really believe that you have nothing to offer the world.

I needed to find Ron to share the conversation with him but he was still missing.

I walked around the singing campfire circle and then I spotted him. Beatrice was sitting on a chair and Ron was stooped over behind her with his arms around her shoulders. He idolised her. I couldn't put my arms around her. This was my birth mother but I hardly knew her. How long would it take for me to get to know her? I watched him and thought, How can he do that? Why is it so easy for him and so hard for me?

I knew the truth: he loved her more than I did.

Mothers' Day

So High

Before we left Coonamble, after Tom's twenty-first, we had nearly convinced Beatrice to come to Newcastle for a holiday. I was ecstatic when she rang one day and said she was ready to catch the coach and would arrive about ten o'clock in the morning. The coach connected with the train at Dubbo. I waited hour after hour for the train to pull into Broadmeadow railway station. She wasn't on any of the trains from Sydney. I sat at the station until dark. Ron finally rang the police in Coonamble as we thought something horrible had happened. We got word back that she was overexcited and had meant she was packed ready to leave but that the coach wouldn't arrive until twenty-four hours later.

In total I had spent close to twelve hours waiting on the very platform that I had stepped onto two decades previously. As I had plenty of time to sit and think, I was taking an emotional trip, remembering that day I went for my first train ride without knowing why or where I was going. How peculiar that now at the same station the daughter awaited the arrival of her natural mother.

Beatrice spent a wonderful nine days with us and we truly got to know each other. Ron and I had planned to take her up to the Barrington Tops where Ron's country was, but as we drove over Cardiff, Beatrice held on tight to the door handle and exclaimed, 'Ooh, it's so 'igh.' She was used to the flat country. I had always taken the landscape of Newcastle for granted and didn't notice the hilly suburbs that made up the 'steel city'. Ron decided to postpone our trip to the mountains until the next time Bea came for a visit, as he thought she would be more confident and feel more secure to travel up the steep slopes of his beloved mountains.

Bea brought her twelve-year-old grandson Jamie with her, partly because she didn't want to take the long trip alone and partly because she couldn't move without Jamie accompanying her. He loved his nan more than his own mother and father. Jamie and Darren were the same age, the same height and both were quiet and shy. The cousins had a week to get to know each other.

The second day I drove my guests all over Newcastle showing them the places of interest. As we drove down Hunter Street, the main street leading up to the beach and lighthouse, Jamie stuck his head out of the car window with amazement and said excitedly, 'Look, Nan, skyscrapers,' meaning the office buildings. They were the tallest buildings he had ever seen. Then when I showed them one of our popular beaches, Nobby's Beach, he again commented on the new sight. We travelled around the tourist drive that proceeded along the esplanade from Nobby's Beach to the next beach around the cliff face, Newcastle Beach. At the time we passed by the ocean it was low tide and heaps of broken rocks were visible. Not having seen the beach before, and not recognising it was low tide and only seeing the numerous rough and jagged rocks, Jamie yelled, 'Look, Nan, earthquake!'

During the next few days, I proudly showed them Lake Macquarie and the vineyards due west from Newcastle. They couldn't get over how we had everything so close to our house, as the nearest town to Coonamble was one hour's drive away and the geography of the surrounding country was so similar; but here in Newcastle it was full of hills and the lake at the same time. I myself saw the town in a new, refreshing way and I realised from a tourist perspective that there were many lovely places to see and enjoy.

We spent a few hours at the RAAF base on the Tuesday. It was a forty-minute drive north-east from our suburb to a little place called Williamtown. Here I allowed my guests to watch in awe the powerful blast of the Mirage jets taking off and coming in for landing practice. Jamie was intrigued and a little frightened. Their eyes of wonder were reward enough for me.

Unfortunately Ron had to work overtime. There was a rush order and he was scheduled for twelve-hour shifts. This meant he could only spend a few hours at night with Bea. He was wonderful with her and joked how it was unfair that he had to have two mothers-in-law. The two of them got on so well it was beautiful to see. Ron didn't see her as a coloured person. Bea called him 'Son'. She also loved how our boys called her 'Nana-Bea'. She said, 'They got respect.' We raised them to give us lots of hugs and kisses before going to bed at night and she loved it when they wished her goodnight in this manner. It was a loving way to end the day. She said that I was the only young mother she knew who read Bible stories to them and prayed as I tucked them into bed.

Beatrice commented every day to Ron that I was a good mother and that she could see how much I loved them. I kissed them so frequently as they were everything to me and I was glad to hear that someone could see my love for them. I always seemed to fail at so many things but loving my children was easy.

I kept Darren home from school for a couple of days as I thought it was more important for him to get to know this side of our family. Also Jamie needed company and the two boys played well together. I was happy playing host to my guests and travelling from place to place gave many opportunities for Bea and me to converse in a non-threatening environment.

On the Thursday, I took Beatrice up to Mum's as Beatrice had told me she would love to see her again. Driving to Mum's, I thought and wondered what the two women would say to each other. How would I feel if I raised a child and that child brought her natural mother to meet me? Mum's kitchen window faced the side street and enabled her to keep a watchful eye for our Torana. When we arrived, my little German mum came out of the house and ran up the path to meet us, her arms outstretched. Smiling and teary-eyed, she hugged me and kissed my forehead saying, 'Donnie, we've got enough love for her too, haven't we?' Yes, I nodded. The two women warmly greeted each other with an endearing hug, then kissed each other. Mum then invited us both inside, where they sat in the lounge room and began to tell each other their life stories.

It was a relaxed atmosphere. I left them alone, observing them from the kitchen as I made a cuppa for everyone. It was odd seeing my two mothers sitting at the same table. Their lives were so different, so opposite. One was rich, the other poor. One black, the other white. One educated, the other not. One able to bear children and the other unable.

As I made afternoon tea, Mum came into the kitchen and said quietly, 'Donna, you shouldn't call her Beatrice – she's your mother. You shouldn't call her that. Please don't call her Beatrice. You mustn't offend her.' I suppose that's what I was waiting for, Mum's blessing. Now I knew what had been holding me back. I didn't want to offend Mum. She raised me as her own. She was loving, generous and we never argued about anything. The last thing I wanted was for anything to come between our love. But nothing could, as our love was greater.

Beatrice listened to Mum's life story with real interest. How she grew up in Germany, was a trained opera singer, a high school teacher. Bea eagerly heard about the trip in the ship to Australia after the war. She asked Mum how she met Dad and how they came to be fostering a child, so Mum told the story of how she met Dad on the ship coming out to Australia and how they went about adopting a child. Bea then asked Mum, 'Why do you sing gospel songs?' Then Mum shared her fascinating testimony of how she became a Christian. Beatrice's eyes never left Mum's face and I could tell she was listening to every word.

The little cuckoo clock in the kitchen kept reminding us every thirty minutes and all too soon three hours had passed by. It was time to leave. We closed the visit with the three of us singing a few gospel songs. It had been a heart-warming visit and both my mothers had gained answers to decades of unanswered questions and twenty-four years of wondering and imagining what this moment would be like.

As we left the house Mum and Bea were talking about the garden and about how much they both enjoyed flowers and pottering around in the yard. I sat in the car waiting for the women to say farewell and their words have left an imprint in my heart for always.

Mum started: 'Beatrice, it's been so lovely to see you again.'

'Oh, it was good. I like your singin,' replied Beatrice adding, 'maybe we'll sing together one day.'

'Who knows,' said Mum.

Beatrice looked straight into Mum's eyes and said softly, 'I just want to thank you.'

'Thank me. For what?' asked Mum, curious and surprised.

'Thank you for doing such a good job with Donna.'

'You don't have to thank me,' replied Mum. 'That's her choice. She chose who she wants to be.'

'Well, I still want to thank you. I could never have done that.'

'Don't make me cranky! I only did what you would have done. I loved her. On the contrary, I should thank you. If you never gave up your child, I would never have been able to enjoy a child.'

It was a sacred moment. Three hearts were united by unconditional love. It truly was Mothers' Day. It was history. They stood there embracing one another, while I tried to remain composed. I was happy, sad, proud and relieved all at once.

On the drive home, Beatrice said, 'What an interesting lady – she's lovely.'

I said, 'Yes, they were very good to me. They loved me very much.' I was so thankful they liked each other. It made it a lot easier. For the first couple of years it felt like I was being pulled from one to the other, although neither of them placed any pressure on me. It was merely my own perception, or perhaps my guilt. The only way I could explain it was being torn between loyalties. Now I was secure what my role was, and the roles of my two mothers. As we travelled home a song came on the radio with lyrics that danced straight into our hearts. It was a song about reunion. This was another sign that the timing was right for us to come together and get to know one another. The jigsaw puzzle was falling into place a piece at a time, and now I was gradually seeing the picture emerge.

HISTORY REPEATING ITSELF

The next day Beatrice wanted to stay home and have a quiet day, so I sat on the floor playing records. I wanted her to know all my favourite songs. We spent two hours talking music. It was unbelievable, but the very ones I chose, Beatrice informed me, were the very ones that Grandfather and the aunties used to sing around the campfire at night. I thought I just liked them because of the beat or melody but those songs had been imprinted on my subconscious.

Beatrice told me how when she went home from the train station that day, she played records over and over. She named the songs she played. The anger and pain and memory of that day sent Beatrice, and thousands of women like her, into a drinking frenzy, trying to kill the pain. In time, it became an addiction.

I sat frozen at our kitchen table, unable to say anything,

just listening and trying not to feel guilty. Beatrice continued, explaining how she would wake up and think it was a bad dream, but it wasn't, so she would drink more. Her heart was broken. The Aboriginal people thought, 'What gives those white people the right to take our babies away. We wouldn't do that to them.'

Neither of us on that day knew why we were split up but Beatrice explained now that she had received a letter from the Welfare Board ordering her to have all her children at the railway station on 21 April 1960. A Welfare Officer would meet her and take her children to a home. Beatrice came to believe that a nurse at Coonamble Hospital must have contacted the Welfare when her twins were born, three months before that time.

Later, we went to Julie's for lunch. Julie was so kind and friendly with Beatrice, and when we left, Beatrice said, 'She's the nicest white person I ever met.' Julie took a photo of us together, the only photo taken during her visit.

We had both Ron's and my friends popping in to meet Beatrice. We sat up until 1.00 o'clock each morning, talking, trying to piece together a lifetime. Beatrice had a short visit with Aunty Margaret and Uncle Cyril, plus we had a special church service where the closing song was, 'God Be With You Till We Meet Again'.

Ron was unable to get away from work to see Beatrice off on the train. I handed her a letter and told her not to read it until the train pulled out. In it, I told her all the things I couldn't verbalise. How precious her visit was. I thanked her for being so kind to me and Mum at Bero. The train was delayed before it pulled out. Tim, who was sad that she was leaving, ran and hid behind a small brick wall. As the train pulled out from the station, Tim, not wanting to miss seeing her off, came out from hiding, and ran along the length of the platform alongside her window and waving, saying, 'Goodbye, Nana-Bea.'

I stood there frozen and waited until the train was out of sight, about a quarter of a mile away, and then the tears fell like a waterfall. I sat on the platform bench and my heart broke as I relived my own history. Last time it was Mum on the platform waving goodbye and this time it was the daughter waving goodbye to the mother. I had such an empty feeling inside. It was more than a farewell, I had just experienced history repeating itself.

MAKING UP FOR LOST TIME

With each letter, Beatrice and I grew closer, as our letters were full of our likes and dislikes, our families, our favourite music and little bits and pieces of our family jigsaw. Beatrice was really enjoying her Christian walk, and so most of our communication was about our faith, the new things we were learning. How to deal with anger and forgiveness. We shared each other's prayer points and Beatrice always mentioned all the new hymns she was singing. She had a beautiful voice, a gift from heaven, and now she was using it to sing gospel. Beatrice sang at Christian rallies in Coonamble, Gilgandra, Walgett and Wee Waa.

I shared her progress with Mum at Beresfield, and it was a special relationship we all had, a special love for one another. God had given three women this very special love which was healing three women's hearts.

———

At Tom's twenty-first, I had also met my natural father, Merv Morris, from Wee Waa. He was a deep thinker, quiet, and had always been a hard worker all his life, driving trucks, shearing, and picking cotton. I was polite when I met him but didn't feel any particular bonding. He loved kids and drove my boys to a shop and bought them a couple of dollars' worth of lollies. I appreciated his kindness. He fell in love with Beatrice and they were always sweethearts, but they lost contact after all the kids were taken away. Beatrice located Morrie (as he was affectionately called) the same year she found me, so now they were back together making up for lost time, just as Beatrice and I were.

So Shamed

From time to time I was reminded about my promise to my brother Barry but where, I wondered, should I start? I had been told by friends that I had a gift in writing but I never believed them. I was watching a series on the ABC which had John Meillon acting in it. I thought, I'll write to him and ask if he thought I had any ability to write. That way I might get an honest opinion. I phoned the ABC and sent a letter to his address with an outline of whnat I would like to publish and anticipated his reply. I sent the letter some time in winter 1984. When I didn't receive a reply after a few months, I felt so shamed. How did I have the gall to do such a thing? Even though writing a book was my daydream, it seemed to fade into the background while I got on with life and left it at a 'one of these days, I will' dream.

I continued to procrastinate about writing for the next

fifteen months, until I spoke with Beatrice one day and we agreed that she should come to Newcastle for a holiday. During her visit, we could celebrate her birthday and my thirteenth wedding anniversary, but the main purpose of the visit would be to obtain all the family background to start the first chapter.

Two days before Beatrice was due to leave Coonamble, we received word that her blood pressure was too high to travel and so the trip was postponed. I was so disappointed. I felt an urgency to obtain information about my grandfather and grandmother, but I needed Beatrice's help with the history behind the family tree. It wasn't until I entered college later that I gained the confidence to ask questions about my Aboriginal family, and most of the information about Grandfather and Pilliga didn't come together until 1988–1990.

Not Alone

VOLUNTEER

I admired people who were happy and who knew how to speak. I still struggled with keeping conversations but I grew a bit in confidence with each passing year. It took years to gain self-confidence. In March 1986, I felt important when I was welcomed to the team at the Newcastle City Mission as a volunteer. After thirteen years on the kitchen floor, to be instantly placed in an office was so encouraging to me, I felt like I had been given the best job in Newcastle. The unpaid work was very rewarding and exciting but, more importantly, very confronting.

I went to the Mission every Tuesday and Thursday. At first I was mainly observing to learn their approach. In my third week there, the superintendent, Mr Laurie Johnson, asked me to sit in on a welfare meeting. I sat observing, but never spoke. I was so impressed with all the community work being done by the various churches and I knew that this was my field and that somehow I too could be a labourer. In the midst of my thoughts I was interrupted. Every eye was on me. I wished I could crawl under my chair. Brian Elboz, the coordinator of the Toronto Assistance Centre, had directed a question specifically at me.

The blood rushed to my head, my heart was thundering, and I felt like I was going to faint. What should I answer?

Brian had asked, 'Donna, can you tell me something about your people, the Aboriginal culture? It will help all of us. We see how Aboriginal families go home for a funeral. They spend all their pension on petrol or a train fare, so when they get back to Newcastle they haven't got any food, so they come to us for help. What is so important about a funeral?'

I hung my head in shame. Did I have to answer? I shook my head and, very embarrassed, I answered, 'I don't know, I've been raised in the city in a white society and I don't know why, sorry.' I felt so dumb.

First Aboriginal Funeral

I relived that moment in the meeting over and over for the rest of the week. The more I remembered it, the angrier I got with myself. I was so depressed on the Friday night, I knelt beside my bed and sobbed my heart out. I poured my heart out to the Lord because he knew me better than anyone and I could always take my problems to him. I knelt there maybe six or seven minutes, just sobbing, trying to ease my troubled heart. Then I prayed these words: 'Lord, please help me to be a real Aborigine. Help me to become one of them. I'm so ashamed, I didn't know that answer for Brian. Please, Lord, help me to identify to be able to really relate to the Aboriginal people. Make me exactly like them.' I emptied out all my tears of shame and then went to the lounge room, still feeling depressed.

On the Sunday night I found myself lying in bed, crying my heart out again. Ron asked, 'What's wrong?' After some deep breaths I was able to mumble, 'Mum's going to die.' He wrapped his arms around me and lovingly wiped the flow of tears. He tried to comfort me by saying, 'We'll cross that bridge together when the time comes. Now stop thinking about it, you'll only make yourself sick.' I cried myself to sleep. I didn't want to lose Mum from Beresfield. I needed her. The boys needed her. I loved her too much and I wasn't ready to let her go. I had lost Dad in 1975 and I didn't want to lose Mum too.

The next evening I put Mark into bed and was singing him to sleep when the phone rang. Ron came into the room where I was standing, patting Mark's bottom, and laid his hand on my shoulder and quietly said, 'Darl, it's for you — it's Barry. It's bad news.'

As I walked up the hallway I took a deep breath. I knew then: I had the wrong mother. I picked up the phone and said, 'Hello.'

Barry said in his husky voice, 'Sis, I got some bad news.'

As he was saying it I prayed, 'Lord, help Thou me.'

Barry was saying, 'It's Mum, she's gone.'

I told him I already knew. I told him how upset I got the night before. I got the message but I got it mixed up and thought my white mum was going to die.

We had to wait three days before the funeral and during that time the events of the past week swam around in my head. I knew God was going to answer my prayer — somehow. I'd never been to an Aboriginal funeral before and now here I was going to my first, my own mother's.

SAYING GOODBYE

I stood at the front of the little church that was surrounded with very dark Aboriginal people, all wearing
black and white. I felt stupid standing there, as I felt I was
unsuitably dressed, in my light lemon dress and stockings.
All the other women wore black dresses and black stockings.
I stood out: I wished I was invisible. I watched grown men,
women and children crying their hearts out. When I saw
so many children, I wished I had brought my three boys,
but in Newcastle, children didn't go to funerals. It seemed
like I did everything different, but I just didn't know what
to expect.

The aunts were broken-hearted. I stood silently. There
were so many strangers. Barry asked Ron to help carry the
casket inside with the brothers. When he returned to me,
he just broke up and said it was the hardest thing he had
ever had to do. I had a tear here and there, but wondered

why I couldn't cry like the others.

The service was quick. No-one could sing. No-one would hear her tender voice again. It was as if the heart of Coonamble had died. As I gazed at the dark faces, I realised how much they loved her. Ron and I were asked to sit with Morrie in the front pew but I wished we were sitting in the back row. I had worn the wrong colour and people were staring at me. A non-Aboriginal minister took the service, whereas I had expected an Aboriginal minister. The service was the same as in the city, and I'd expected it to be different.

As families and friends organised lifts to the cemetery, I noticed a broken-hearted boy trying to hide beside a high overgrown shrub. I went up to him as I recognised him as young Jamie, sobbing his heart out. I cuddled him as I knew how he loved and idolised his Nana. My heart went out to all the children crying. Jamie was beside himself with grief. I caught Widdy's eye and motioned for him to come over and console Jamie but he was in the depths of grief and unable to move. When Jamie was five years old he chose to live with his Nana and she virtually raised him. I knew that this day was devastating for a twelve-year-old. I felt guilty as I watched adult after adult crying, overcome by grief. They knew Beatrice better than her own daughter did. There were lots of issues I was feeling guilty about.

I had never seen such a big funeral. Car after car. Ordinary sedans had six people in them, buses were loaded. The local traffic stopped as a mark of respect, even the interstate truckies. White people took off their hats as we drove past. People walking over the bridge stopped until we passed by. Ron and I were touched by their sensitivity. It was so kind. I had never seen such respect in the city. As we turned the corner at the cemetery turn-off, I glanced back only to see car after car and even more cars still coming over the bridge. I counted seventy cars in the cortège. So many people gathering for a funeral, coming from all over New South Wales.

When we gathered around the grave, my sister Tom gave me a blue rose to place on the coffin with my brothers and sisters. Not knowing what to do, I just watched for them to move. The women were wailing now. Morrie and I stood side by side and Ron held my hand, standing behind me. Everyone's eyes were fixed on the grave. No-one spoke. After some time Morrie picked up some dirt and sprinkled it over the grave and softly said, 'Well, goodbye Mum.' I said to myself, 'Goodbye, Mother.' Within fifteen minutes it was all over and people left quickly. The aunts went to visit Grandmother's, Grandfather's and Aunty Dot's graves. Ron sat in the car crying his heart out.

My People

I sat in my mother's backyard an hour later with all the relations and felt something begin to stir within my heart. Something was happening, but I didn't know what. About fifteen minutes later all I could remember was that I kept looking from one face to another. I looked at a child, then an elder, at a male, then a female. I studied the faces. I noticed dark ones and fairer ones. Then slowly, slowly, the tears started to roll down my cheeks. The more I examined the faces the more it made me cry. It was so wonderful. I felt something I had never felt before. I saw true beauty in each face I beheld.

All of my anger and denial left at that moment. All the pain I had carried within me all my life left and in an instant I fell in love with a whole race of people. My spirit danced for joy. I felt new and wonderful in a strange way, and I began to understand that something spiritual had happened. I said to my heart, 'These people are so beautiful, these wonderful people, and to think, they are my relations. My people. I belong to them.' I whispered, 'Thank you, God.'

We had buried my mother seven years after she received my letter. Seven years to the very day, in fact to the very hour she'd opened it, the day before Mother's Day. When she read my letter I gave back meaning to her life and now that she had died she gave my life meaning.

I wept with thanks as I sat there silently praising God for yet another miracle of love. Another answered prayer. He made me Aboriginal but all my life I was unable accept His blessing. Now, for the first time in my life, I eagerly received what He had bestowed on me. This was the day my head and heart were in unison over my identity. The tears that flowed were full of guilt and shame. I now understood what the barriers had been and why I had been cautious. Although in recent years I was able to admit I was Aboriginal, it was only head knowledge and not flowing from my spirit or my heart. Apart from Mum, Ron and my boys, I protected myself by never allowing anyone to get too close to me because I was convinced that sooner or later they would reject me.

I could see now that from day one these people had wanted to be close to me but they were more perceptive than I, and had allowed me room and time to draw nearer to them. At last that day came and I wanted to get close to them. I claimed them as my relations and from that time they were my people. As I sat looking at their dark velvet skin, I knew that this too had been another barrier, as somewhere in my childhood I had adopted the view from white society that the fairer the skin the more acceptable people were; but now the darker their skin, the deeper the love I had for them.

I had an overwhelming sense of belonging. I had been searching for something all my life but didn't know what I was searching for until this moment and now it was so easy to identify. I needed to know what I belonged to. I needed to know that I was a part of a family and I needed to know I was a part of a race. It was much more than just needing to know, it was a matter of wanting to belong as well as feeling I belonged. I became one of them and they became my people. I could now say I was Aboriginal knowing it was coming from my heart and not just my head. I thought about the events of the past two weeks, how ashamed I was not knowing the importance of a funeral. Now I knew it was more than a funeral: it was a farewell, a celebration of life, a returning to the land and a family reunion. I knew my prayer had been answered. I became one of my race.

MY MOTHERS

We returned home to Newcastle five hours after the funeral accompanied by my brother Sooty and his little girl, who were going to sleep overnight and catch the early train to Sydney the following day.

Sooty, a private person, was quiet and thoughtful for most of the journey. When he spoke it was in a very soft tone. He seemed dejected all weekend. He shared a couple of little stories about our mother which I listened to eagerly; it was very important to me to learn as much as possible about her. I was so aware that I really didn't know her very well and I needed to satisfy my curiosity. Sooty had been fostered out and had come home when he was fifteen. Coming home isn't as easy as one might anticipate. You come home and you know that the people are your family but you also know you have lost a whole lifetime, and in a very real sense they are strangers. But you try to carry on as if nothing has happened and this makes adjustment a difficult emotional transition. From what Sooty had told us I felt he had a sense of regret that he missed the chance to get close to our mother or at least really get to know her. I suspect he also had to work through issues affecting his personality.

Lying in bed that night I reminisced about the card and the first letter I sent home just in time for Mother's Day. How short seven years seemed now. Having Sooty and his daughter stay with us helped to fill some of the void I felt as I woke on this Mother's Day, 1986. Both Sooty and I felt the cloud that overshadowed this year's Mother's Day. Ron and I saw Sooty and his daughter off at the train station. We told him how much it meant to us having him stay one night with us, and we invited him to come up for the weekend so we could continue to get to know one another.

As Sooty had left by nine o'clock, I was able to make it to church for the eleven o'clock service but found it extremely difficult sitting in the pew trying to be cheerful. Although I'd hardly wept at the funeral the day before, today I couldn't stop the tears from falling as I sat thinking about my two mothers. I sat with Julie and I knew she was also feeling my loss. She knew both my mothers, she knew what I had been through in the past seven years, and she was moved with compassion as we both tried to deal with the present. The more I tried to subdue my grief the more emotional I became, and in the end I had to go outside the building and have a good cry. Julie came and hugged me – she knew the pain I was dealing with.

When I returned to my seat I refused to listen to the

guest speaker who kept talking about his beloved mother. It was difficult for me as the sting of death was so fresh and sharp; I suppose the minister would have had more sensitivity had he known what I had gone through the day before. I tried not to listen to the numerous stories he recalled about his mother yet couldn't help but feel anger and envy that he at least knew his mother, so to help me focus on something else I sat quietly and read psalm after psalm. I kept reading one after another trying to find comfort. Then a verse stood out and it carried me through the rest of the day. It said: 'Precious in the sight of the Lord is the death of His saints.'

Being Mother's Day, in the afternoon Ron, the three boys and I visited Mum at Beresfield. Mum was so understanding and so moved with compassion that when we arrived she lovingly held me in her kitchen and we wept together.

I had driven to Mum's house the day after Barry had told us that Beatrice had passed away. I wanted to tell Mum personally – it wasn't the type of news to repeat over the phone. Even though I gave Mum the message three times, she couldn't understand what I was saying. Bea's death was so sudden and unexpected that when she grasped the message she sat at her table crying in disbelief. She began hitting the table and sobbing, saying, 'Oh my God, why? Why, Lord? You should have taken me, I'm an old woman. You should have left Beatrice here for Donna.' Mum and I had sat crying together at the table. I sat feeling awkward, not knowing what to say. I didn't know what Mum's reaction would be but I hadn't expected her to say something so loving. But Mum was a special person, never selfish, always putting others first, and all my life she showed me what real love was. There is no higher act of love than wanting to lay down your life for someone else. That was real love and that's why she was a special mum.

NOT ALONE

The first two weeks of mourning I spent like everyone else, I guess, remembering conversations and scenes, and crying, and working through anger. I remember sitting in my lounge room and feeling isolated, cut off from the family. I envied the relations in Coonamble, being all together sharing stories, laughing, singing and grieving together. I needed to be with them. My loss was compounded by the guilt I was feeling about not loving Bea the way I should have; I had held back to protect myself and now I had to deal with my conscience. Ron was very understanding. He knew I liked having space when I silently dealt with things and he knew I had to work through all the pain. He cared a lot but as I was a reserved person he gave me what I wanted – time and space.

On Wednesday, 19 May 1986, about two weeks after the funeral, I recall sitting at my dining table having morning tea after all the boys had gone to school. I just sat thinking and silently conversing with the Lord. The best way I could come to terms with my bereavement was through prayer. As I sat at my table crying and working through my anger, I unloaded all my doubts and self-pity to the Lord. I then asked for a sign that I might know I wasn't alone in these days of sorrow.

I thought I had only been sitting there for about half an hour but when I checked the time I was surprised to learn I had been there for exactly two hours. I decided I had best make up for the time out, and went to the laundry to commence a load of washing even though I wasn't motivated for housework. As I packed the clothes in the washing machine I felt tired and weak from crying. As I waited for the water to fill the bowl, I heard a noise above that of the passing traffic and the other usual neighbourhood noises. It pricked my ears. I slowly walked outside to the top of the ramp which met our back door and stood quietly listening and waiting for it again. It confirmed what I thought I'd heard. There it was again. It was coming from a bird sitting in my next-door neighbour's mulberry tree. The call of the currawong, calling to me.

What was so special about that? Well, as I mentioned, in my childhood days when we lived at the camp, these birds would wake us each morning, at least fifty currawongs singing their melodious morning song. The only other time I heard that bird call was when Ron took me to Gundy to stay at Aunty Lorna and Uncle Vince's property. All these years I'd been living in the city and had never heard a currawong at our house, as we lived on the main road and the traffic would have frightened them away. This was my sign that I wasn't alone. I stood there on the ramp with tears of happiness. I thanked God for answering my prayer so quickly. I couldn't be in Coonamble so He sent me a beautiful currawong to be with me. That big hollow feeling in my stomach and that pit of loneliness disappeared and a warm feeling came over me instead. I wasn't alone at all.

THE LETTER

Mourning or Sorry Time, as Koori people call it, takes up much of your time and uses a lot of energy, as you are preoccupied with the loss and filled with questions. It's the unanswered questions that bring frustration and the guilt that produces anger and regret. For me, I felt guilt about not identifying with my people and my regret concerned the loss of a heritage.

The next day was Thursday, 20 May 1986. Although I had a sense of not being alone, once again I was having difficulty concentrating on my housework because I was still consumed with anger and guilt. I knew I had to move on but anger and confusion were clouding my vision and holding me back. I couldn't progress past the 'why' question. I couldn't understand why God reunited Beatrice and myself, nor could I understand why He had to take her so suddenly, especially now at this crucial time when Bea was going to enlighten me about my grandparents' history, about our family tree and about her life.

I needed this information for the book and as Bea and I had become friends it seemed timely to commence. I was sorry that I'd wasted so many years procrastinating. The grieving process made me feel like I had come to a stop sign and I couldn't move forward. I knew I had to hand over my anger and guilt to the Lord as this would free me and allow me to move on past this point of time. So I knelt beside my bed and took it to the one who is greater than I. As I knelt and prayed from the depth of my agony I cried, 'Lord, I don't understand why you took Beatrice now especially when we were really getting to know each other. I really wanted to write our story but it's pointless now. Lord, if it's your will I write this book, as a sign, let someone say to me in the next seven days that I have a gift in writing and I should write the book. If no-one says this I will know it was my will and I'm not meant to do it. Show me Thy way.'

On the first day a friend called Bev Chapman phoned and enquired how I was getting on. I told her about the funeral and meeting all the relations and how I felt at ease with them and how I felt a part of the family. I never mentioned anything about how I had given up the desire to write a book. Bev then remarked, 'Donna, you have to write the book now to make sense of your mother's death.' I dismissed it as coincidence. The next day I received a sympathy card from Julie, and on the inside she had written, 'Donna, write the book now. It is a lovely story and it has to be told.' Again I dismissed it. On the fourth day another friend, Vivianne, visited and again with no prompting she said, 'Donna, now more than ever you must write a book.

It will help you heal.' But because these were my closest friends who knew how keenly I had anticipated Bea's visit and why it was so significant to me, I didn't allow any of their comments to influence me, so I didn't believe this was the sign I had prayed for.

With the funeral and bereavement I had taken a few weeks off from my volunteer work at the City Mission but as I was trying to get back to some normality, I decided that my first steps would be to return to the Mission the following week. So on Thursday 27 May I resumed my duties. It was 'back' week and we were very busy as people on pensions were only paid once a fortnight then, and on that back week we always had lots of clients who had run out of food and who needed our assistance to help them get through until the next pension day.

All day I completely dismissed my prayer request and actually overlooked that this had been the seventh day in which I had asked to receive a sign which would impact upon my future and the direction of the book. Ron was on twelve-hour shifts at the dockyard, so when I arrived home from work I automatically checked the letterbox. There were a couple of sympathy cards and a personal letter in a blue envelope addressed to me. I didn't recognise the hand-writing so I gently opened the seal as I walked from the letterbox to the verandah. I read through the letter so excit-edly and quickly that I had to reread it to make sure I hadn't misunderstood. I stood there reading the most wonderful letter that I had ever received in my life. I couldn't believe my news. I stood on the verandah but I wanted to shout the good news to the world.

It was a letter from Mr John Meillon. First of all he

apologised for taking so long to reply to my letter. Then he gave me some constructive criticism and encouraged me to write a book. He wrote, 'Donna, you indeed have a gift in writing, and it is a lovely women's story. Write a short story and send it to *Woman's Day*, as a book is hard work. An astute filmmaker may read it and be interested in it.' A film had been my secret dream that I never trusted with anyone, but God knew my secret thoughts. I read the letter over and over. The very dream I was prepared to relinquish had been approved. I wept with joy that God had once again blessed me and given me back my dream with His blessing.

Ron was amazed at the letter when he read it later that night. I had to explain to him how I had written to Mr Meillon fifteen months previously and how I felt really ashamed when he didn't reply within six months. I hadn't even had the confidence to share my thoughts and dreams with my own husband, as I thought I was stupid and I didn't want him to laugh at my silly ideas. This was a reflection of society's expectations for Aboriginal people, that said we were dumb, dirty and lazy, that we would never learn. I had picked up that message as a child and even as an adult I still believed it. I didn't need my husband or others to laugh at my dreams or to tell me, 'You'll never do it.'

I must have read the letter ten times that night. It was too good to be true. I phoned my friends and shared my news with them and they rejoiced with me. They asked, 'Why did you write to him?' I explained how I was just moved as I watched him acting in the series *The Fourth Wish* and how I simply followed my heart by writing to him to obtain an unbiased opinion. It was a wonderful thing Mr Meillon did, taking the time to reply to an unknown person. It restored my faith in human nature.

Perhaps he remembered someone encouraging him when he was young. In his letter he had also explained how he had been busy making three films in the past fifteen months, including *Crocodile Dundee*. He actually had written the letter on Mother's Day and didn't post it off until a week later. He remembered to mail it on the Wednesday and I had received it on the Thursday, the seventh day of my prayer request. My heart rejoiced. My spirit was soaring. My dream had been handed back giftwrapped in gold. It was the most wonderful gift I had ever received. 'Tell me the desires of thy heart and I will give thee thy desires.'

Becoming

WOLLOTUKA

My days at the City Mission were valuable as I was learning a lot about life outside the church. I was interacting with the poor, the lonely, with ex-prisoners and those with drug dependencies, and was confronting issues which I'd never thought about; I also began a six-month study on what unconditional love meant. I believed I was meant for welfare work and I enjoyed my two days at the Mission. I looked forward to my work and to learning about different lifestyles, and I was surprised by how I loved the people as well as the work.

The superintendent, Mr Laurie Johnson, and the secretary, Mrs Wendy Raine, were a wonderful team and great role models. They taught me so much and I love them for the faith they had in me, as they always encouraged me to take another step in my personal development. Laurie suggested I enroll at TAFE and do the Certificate in Welfare as it would help me understand theory and it would also benefit the Mission. I never believed I would be able to do such a course, having left school when I was fifteen and always believing I was too dumb.

With each passing day I became increasingly aware how ignorant I was about my people, our ways and our culture. I longed to know more about them, but how? In July, about two months later, I overheard a report on the local news about an Aboriginal Bridging Course, Wollotuka, which was to commence at the Advanced College of Higher Education; if anyone was interested, they were to come in and speak to the coordinator the next day.

I realised then that I could be a go-between. I thought, yes, I can be a bridge: all my life I was white and now I was learning the black way. So the next day I went to speak with the coordinator and see what the course entailed. The coordinator from Wollotuka, Lorraine Thomas, organised an interview with Mr Morland, the Head of the Welfare Department, who asked me a series of questions. One key question was, Did I read? I was thankful that I had immersed myself in books during the past seven years and when I was asked to name some of the authors I was able to recite at least twelve of my favourite authors. Before I knew what had happened I was accepted and I had signed on the dotted line. I had not only enrolled for the Bridging Course, but also the Associate Diploma of Social Welfare.

The six-month Bridging Course was a prerequisite into mainstream entry. I didn't really understand it all, so I signed an enrolment, perhaps under false pretences, as I only planned to stay six weeks for the Aboriginal Studies in the Bridging Course as well as completing the sociology strand, as they were looking at Aborigines in Australian society today. That's all I wanted to know. Then I would leave.

I really wanted to be a teacher but the Diploma in Education was a four-year course and that time frame scared me off. Welfare was my second option as it was only two years. Not that I had any intention of staying – I would be out of there before they got to know me. Right now I had such a hunger for knowledge about my people. As part of the entrance exam I had to write one page on why I decided to do the course. I was guided by my heart and wrote the truth and I was accepted. I don't know where the words came from as I normally didn't talk about 'blacks' or 'whites' but the words on paper read: 'I've realised that if I am to succeed in a white man's world I have to have the piece of paper to prove I am formally educated.' Mr Morland accepted my answers and I was accepted. It happened so fast.

When Ron came home from work that night he asked, 'What did you do today?'

I said dumbly, 'I think I signed away two years of my life.' Neither Ron nor I believed I could do it. I reassured myself by saying, 'I'm only staying six weeks anyhow.' I was so excited that we would be doing Aboriginal Studies and this had been the bait that I needed.

In order to do a full-time course at college it meant I had to leave my part-time work at the City Mission. I had only been there for four months but I had grown as a person and as a Christian. They were sorry to lose me but I promised I would come in during vacations and the Christmas break so it wasn't goodbye. In between office duties I would talk to the volunteers and get to know what type of service they were providing. I particularly liked

assisting two wonderful elderly ladies who had been keen
volunteers for many many years distributing toys for dis-
advantaged children. Sorting out the toys really brought
home the Christmas spirit and made it a special time for
the workers as well as the clients.

I got to know some of the dear homeless men who
came in every day for a hot lunchtime meal. It was hard
to understand why people didn't want to look after their
own father or husband. I couldn't help but be confused as
to why they were abandoned. We used to have young
men who were sentenced by the courts to do their community hours at the City Mission. One of them who had
completed his six weeks and had to appear in court the
next day overheard me telling Wendy that I always cut my
husband's hair, so he asked me to cut his so he would look
more respectable for court. When I was almost finished
one of the homeless men also asked me to cut his hair as
he too had his court appearance the next day. By now I
had learned to communicate with people from different
walks of life and as we talked I asked this gentle man why
he was going to court. He replied, somewhat embarrassed,
yet also in a proud tone, even boastful, 'Well, love, it's
like this. I'm a flasher and I got caught and now I've been
charged with indecent exposure or something.' It was a bit
embarrassing yet at the same time it was funny. These were
real people who put a face to the term 'welfare work'. I
developed a sense of humour which became a vital survival
skill. In just six months, I had also acquired a love for the
poor and lonely, and enjoyed being their friend as well as
learning some valuable skills.

I remember I was typing one day in the office when a

fair-skinned woman with greeny-blue eyes poked her head around the office door and asked me, 'Oh, are you a Murray?' I said, 'No. I'm a Meehan.' I thought she was referring to surnames. I saw this woman again at college as she was also enrolled in the Bridging Course. I learned she was Aboriginal and from Queensland. Cathy remembered me from the Mission and told me that up north the Aboriginal people are known as Murris.

I was so ashamed when I found this out at college but everyone else thought it was so funny. Somehow laughing with this group was different and instead of laughing at things I found I was laughing with them. There was so much to learn here. The first thing was that we called ourselves Koories and people with white skin Gubbas. This came about with the early settlement when the first contact our people had was with white people who predominantly represented the government. As we couldn't pronounce some of the consonants we adapted the language so government became gubbament, hence the word gubba. From this I learned a whole new vocabulary but as well as acquiring a new Koori language, at the same time I had to adhere to the vocabulary recognised by the institution. These were informative days and I enjoyed the mental stimulation along with the Aboriginal interaction.

With the demands of my studies and the time-consuming research for assignments, after four months I had to leave the Mission until the Christmas break. I would be seeing Wendy at college from time to time as she was doing the same Diploma, but part-time to cater for her full-time employment. I also knew I would be seeing the new superintendent, Graham Gordon, frequently as he and Ron had a mutual interest in CB radio. Graham and I had become good friends so when I left I gave him a gift of a coffee mug which had a verse of scripture on it plus a lovely painted picture of the sunrise over the sea. I think it was simply symbolic of a new dawning for me.

CULTURE SHOCK

I t took my mother's death to make me realise my heritage. Losing her made me comprehend just how much I had lost. Now I had a hunger for knowledge, an urgent need to acquire information about Aboriginal history. I knew that I did indeed belong to this race but I felt very, very insignificant. It was this realisation that I knew nothing about Aboriginal culture that had motivated me to enrol at college.

My biggest obstacle was the financial hurdle. For the past year I had been ironing for working women and had ten regular clients. I had met Vivianne through the CB club and she was a professional ironer. Vivianne showed me how to iron properly and how to fold the clothes as professionals did and so I started taking in a little work. This money enabled me to send Mark to preschool as I couldn't otherwise afford the daily fee. I only sent him on Mondays to try to loosen the apron strings and to prepare him for school the following year. Preschool was a totally new concept for me, but as Mark had such an attachment to me I decided it was worth a try.

For the other four days a week he played in the lounge room while I ironed day and night. At times I was ironing until three o'clock in the morning but the work gave me such satisfaction, plus I felt I was contributing towards the family purse and this was very gratifying. However, with college lectures I no longer had the time to continue my little business.

When I was informed I was eligible for ABSEC, financial assistance the government provided similar to AUSTUDY, I couldn't believe it. Everything was falling into place as if it was meant to be. Wow. If I had known that the government would pay me to get educated I might have jumped in years ago, except it wasn't the right timing. In reality I had to experience all the pain from my life which provided a clearer and deeper insight into not only myself but also society, thus giving me the driving force towards my education.

I was having second thoughts as I walked towards the main entrance on my first day of the Bridging Course, as I told myself I'd probably be the oldest person in the class. Here I was, thirty-two years old, and returning to school. As I neared the front entrance to the humungous brick building I overheard a conversation between two women in front of me who were walking in the same direction. One was filled with excitement at having been accepted into college. I heard her comment to the other woman how she had retired from the workforce five years previously and found retirement monotonous, so she applied to undertake her Bachelor of Arts degree and was jubilant that she had been admitted. She was seventy years old, and I found myself being caught up in her enthusiasm, so after that I didn't feel old.

The first few weeks were exciting and it was a new experience for me to be surrounded by Aboriginal people. I listened to the other students talking about their childhood and life experiences. I felt like the new kid on the block again. I listened and silently compared my life to that of the other students.

Being at college made me aware of how much I had been protected in my upbringing. One of the first concepts we learned was that of control, and I soon realised how much I had been in control of my life. If I didn't like what was on TV or the radio, I could just turn it off, however at college I was exposed to the views of the world, to differing moral views on a wide range of topics, to things like offensive language, and even new, weird hairstyles. It was obvious that many students preferred to wear black clothing and I actually felt depressed in this new environment. I was very secure at home being in control, but here it was all too confronting – it was indeed a culture shock for me.

TIME TO RECONSIDER

I t was the challenge to my own values and belief system
that threatened me more than the high education expec-
tancy level. After three weeks I thought I was in the wrong
boat, so I resigned. I was comfortable being at home again.
Cooking, cleaning, and being available for my sons. For two
weeks I washed windows, ironed, sewed and played
mummy. I prayed about it every day and my argument was,
'Lord, I shouldn't be wasting two years in college, there's
too much work to do in the community now.'

Two years previously, I had completed a few courses at
Lifeline in Newcastle. On the first day I was drawn to a very
shy woman in our group. I felt compelled to befriend her. Her
name was Bev Grono, from Munmorah. Our families became
very close and we became like sisters. Bev even resembled my
sister Jayne, and I felt there was some Aboriginality in her
family tree. Our friendship was to span decades.

When I resigned from college Bev came to visit for a couple of hours. Ron was at home as he had resigned from the dockyard six months previously. We sat around the dining table discussing our personal situations and when the topic of college came up I quickly brushed it off. I said, 'I love being at home.' As Ron and Bev continued talking I had an awful feeling come over me. I went to my bedroom and knelt beside my bed and prayed about it. I knew what this awful feeling was, I knew that I wasn't in God's will. I prayed, 'Lord, I don't want to go there.' Nothing happened. I still felt stressed and knotted inside. No peace came. I cried, then prayed again, 'Lord, I'm happy at home. I hate it there, the language, the people.' I sobbed. I just leaned on the bed silently praying, 'Don't make me go back.' I waited . . . but still no peace came.

Then with a sorrowful heart I submitted: 'Lord, if it's Your will I go to college, as a sign get them to ring me up. If they don't I will know I can stay home.' As I went back to my guest I felt happier as I knew it would never happen. The college would never ring. Students drop out every day so they wouldn't miss one more.

Half an hour later the phone rang. It was Lorraine Thomas, the coordinator from Wollotuka. She said, 'I was just sitting here thinking about you. Come back.' I was surprised but said, 'No, I can't.' Lorraine tried to convince me but I only wanted to be in my four safe walls. I returned to Ron and Bev, not telling them about the phone call, dismissing it as coincidence.

The phone rang again and this time it was Joan Peters from the Aboriginal Education Unit in Brown Street, Newcastle. She asked me to reconsider and go back to college. She told me she knew I could do the work. I cried because it made me so sad, it was the last thing I wanted. I just wanted to stay in control at home, but I was being 'called'. So after the weekend I returned to college to give it another go. Six weeks later I found myself having the same doubts again. I reasoned with myself: I shouldn't be here, it's a waste of time. I'm needed now, there's too much work to do in the community. Who needs a piece of paper? Haunted by these thoughts I prayed as I dropped my first assignment in the tray. 'Lord, if it's Your will that I should be here, as a sign, let me get a distinction in my first assignment. If I don't, I know I can stay at home.'

I knew it was impossible. I would never get a distinction. I had left school at fifteen and I barely knew how to use the library, let alone write an essay. As I walked to the car park I was actually delighted at the prospect of being on the kitchen floor again.

Our sociology lecturer was Mr Phil Vaile. As he handed back the assignments two weeks later, I reminded myself about my prayer. I took a breath, opened up the front page, and wept with disappointment as I saw the words, 'High Distinction, impressive research, well constructed and fascinating topic.' I had written about CB radio, the only thing I knew. Not only did Phil talk about my assignment, but he selected the six most interesting papers and asked us to present them to the class explaining why we chose the topic, how we researched it, and giving the references for our assignments. I could not believe my results. I wondered, How on earth did this happen? This meant I would have to stay at college.

We had been warned that our first written examination was coming up in four weeks' time. I was nervous at the prospect because I had a problem retaining information. I spent each Saturday and Sunday afternoon rereading the sociology lectures but there was so much to remember. I had read all the lecture notes six times. I couldn't memorise them, words and quotes were swimming around in my head.

The night before the big exam I thought I'd finish tea, put the boys to bed then study till midnight. At 9.30 we got a call on the CB radio from one of our friends. He wanted to commit suicide. Ron and I drove to his house and spent four hours with him trying to talk him out of it. He had locked himself in his bedroom with a rifle. He was drunk, depressed and under medication for cancer. He had no wife, his children were in trouble, he was in financial difficulties, and he'd had a blue with his only mate. He was lonely, alone and very angry.

Another close friend of the family was also at the scene but every suggestion we made only agitated our frustrated friend. It seemed like we couldn't help him. We eventually contacted Lifeline, who suggested we call an ambulance for assistance.

So at 1.00 am we called in the ambulance; the ambulance driver also found a sharp carving knife under the driver's seat of our friend's car. He was admitted to hospital for the night for observation until he was no longer a threat to himself or his family. I crawled into bed at 2.00 am and as I dropped off to sleep I thought: If I fail tomorrow's test I don't care because saving a friend's life is far more important. As I drove to college in the morning I wasn't even nervous. As we stood in single file outside the exam room, my only concern was for our friend. I listened to the various conversations. People stressing out, swearing, smoking, trying to memorise definitions. I just stood praying for my friend.

When I was handed the exam paper, in all honesty my pulse didn't change. I quickly worked through the five-page test and went back to the questions I didn't know and tried my best at answering them. I was guided by trigger words and familiar phrases and all in all I did my best. I hoped I would pass – anything over a pass would be a bonus, anyway if I failed I had a good excuse. The results would be posted on a board outside the sociology faculty room the following fortnight.

Two weeks later, I held my breath as I stood waiting for the students to check the noticeboard. I couldn't believe it when I learned I had managed a credit pass. I had come fifth in place out of the sixty students, so I was ecstatic. Everything was simply falling into place. I knew now I was meant to do welfare. Up until that point I was saying, 'I'll prove it to white society that I can do it, or I'll prove to my husband I'm not stupid,' but now I realised I had to prove it to myself first.

It was great having Aboriginal friends for the first time in my life and I loved hearing about their life experiences on the missions. I met Koories from all over New South Wales. Ron and Mum were a great support for me, as when I had doubts they would always come back with a positive remark and encourage me on. I had a good tutor, Kelly, and would discuss with her what concepts the lecturer wanted in assignments, but I did all the research and typed the assignments. I had a new role and the boys were aware of it and eventually accepted how much time it consumed. I would take them to the park and sit reading in the sun while they occupied themselves with each other.

It was a demanding workload. I managed to take Mum

shopping on Saturday, teach Sunday School, and assist with the junior youth group at our church on Tuesday nights. David Copas was the leader and I assisted with stories, craft and games. Trying to keep house, home, church and studies left little time for sleep and socialising. At times my house looked like a bomb had hit it. Many, many times I felt ashamed how I had judged Aunty Lorna for having a messy house – but hers was nothing to what my house looked like during my studies.

A PLACE FOR LEARNING

I felt isolated without any Christian support at college so I asked the Lord to show me where were the Christians. The Aboriginal enclave was a small room tucked away under the stairs of the main student cafeteria. One day I sat talking to an older Koori man who asked me, 'Would you like to see my résumé?' I'd never heard the word before, and I had no idea what he was talking about. But not wanting to sound dumb I said yes. He handed me a book with references in it. I read all about this man. His people were from Bundjalung near Casino. He was Ken McBride, now living in Toronto. He was a lay preacher in the Aboriginal church at West Lakes. Again all my fears had vanished; I had support right amongst our own little group.

I did something that made a few of the Koori students cranky with me. They weren't really cranky but they teased me for weeks on end. I thought it was wonderful to have an allowance which enabled me to study, so before we went on Christmas vacation, I wrote a letter of appreciation to DEET in Sydney where all our ABSTUDY forms were processed. I told them how grateful I was for their financial support. I continued, saying that it was too much money and that I only expected $20 a week for petrol to get to college. When I told Lorraine and the students what I had done they weren't impressed and said they would throw me out if their payments were reduced to $20. I had to wear it as they jokingly referred to me as '$20 Donna'.

So ended the first six months at college. I had survived even after buckets of tears and mountains of doubts. I had learned. I learned to appreciate Koori humour but most of all I was being educated about our history. I passed all my assignments with mainly credits and looked forward to the Christmas vacation with my family.

The new academic year commenced in March and with it came another doubtful period. A couple of weeks into the semester I wasn't convinced that Christians should worry about getting qualified. I felt guilty not being able to help others as my studies were so time-consuming. It really burdened me, so after a couple of weeks of praying about it and seemingly getting no answer, as I drove to college one day I thought, Yes, I'm going to leave.

Before I got out of the car I prayed, 'Lord, I'm not sure I'm doing Your will. Please show me it's all right for Christians to get a higher education.' I walked from the car park to the main entrance. As I came to the two front doors there was a notice in large black letters stuck on with Blu-Tack. I read it three times to make sure I wasn't dreaming. The poster read:

Christian Student Body Meeting
12.15 am   Room A112
Guest Speaker: Principal, Swansea Primary School
Topic: 'Christians and Higher Education'

I was floating all day. I was in the centre of God's will. I wasn't alone at college. He was there with me. I spent my lunch break listening to the speaker. After that sign I stopped complaining about being at college. I no longer doubted that I had been called. I committed myself to study, and I worked hard. After I put my boys to bed at 9.00 pm I would commence my studies until 1.00–2.00 am every night for the next two years. Sleep became a luxury.

I couldn't socialise with our friends as I couldn't sacrifice the time. I never knew such a workload or stress, but it was all worth it. I did every assignment on an Indigenous perspective so I was learning our ways, past, present and future directions. I put every assignment together with tears. Reading how Aboriginals were treated, I had to deal constantly with my anger and sorrow. At times I was mentally and physically worn out. I lost myself in old photographs of our people, articles about them, unable to satisfy my hunger for knowledge. I became very sentimental for our people. It was as if I had been called to mourn for them. This was my time to learn.

Your People Will
Be My People

BELONGING

I had a job waiting for me at the City Mission when I completed my studies, but in my second year I just knew I had to work for my people. I had always kept contact with my dear City Mission friends and they understood when I told them I had to work with Aboriginal people. Not that my people needed me, but rather I needed them, I owed them so much. I was trying to make up for all the wasted years in my life. Not meaning my life with my husband or sons, but the years I had wasted not identifying. For one who lived in denial for nearly thirty years, my identity was now so strong, I had truly got my belonging.

I had been guest speaking at numerous schools and churches, sharing my life story as well as the information I had gained at college, and I wanted to work in public relations or in promoting a better understanding of our people. However, I didn't think I would gain employment for such work. In the last few months of study I applied for two positions and went to the interviews but missed out. I was quite disappointed missing these oportunities and resigned myself to the fact that I wouldn't find employment until the new year, because no-one would employ someone in December. I was out of college one week when the phone rang and I was asked if I could start work the following Monday as the Resource Officer for the Awabakal Newcastle Aboriginal Co-op; a month later I became Community Development and Resource Officer.

On the second day on the job the administrator, Mr Jim Wright, welcomed me to the team and very casually said, 'Oh, by the way, you can do the radio program on 2NUR-FM.' As he walked away I thought, I don't know any black music. The radio program was called 'Awabakal Voices', and it went to air for one hour each week. But although I was only on air for one hour, I needed to spend six hours a week just familiarising myself with the music of our people. It was yet another learning adventure.

Within six months I had completed a course at 2NUR which enabled me to do the panelling by myself just like a discjockey. I had people skills and technology wasn't one of my stronger points but I persevered with the panelling and with practice, in time, it became as natural as driving a car. Six months later I was approached by another radio station, Rhema, a new Christian broadcasting station in Newcastle, who asked me to produce a half hour Koori gospel program.

For the first few years all the programs were pre-recorded but I found that the longer I was employed the more needs I perceived and my workload doubled, leaving less time for the radio program which was one of my greatest loves. I soon found there weren't enough hours in the week to fulfil my roles so to save time I began to produce the program live. This was another exhilarating experience as the dynamics were entirely different and people would ring in for a chat or with requests. The greatest challenge I ever encountered was producing Rhema on the graveyard shift. This meant going live to air from midnight until 6.00 am. I needed forty-five minutes until I felt comfortable in the seat and relaxed in a new studio, with new listeners – and at a time when my mind was ready to sleep. I was amazed at how many people were awake in the middle of the night. I spoke to many sick people and a couple of uni students. The time went so quickly, the hours just flying past. It only seemed like I was there for three hours and then I was signing off air. I had a thirty-minute drive home, just made it, then crawled into bed exhausted.

During those years I listened to the various male and female artists and the lyrics they sang made me aware of the enormous array of Aboriginal talent. Although the Awabakal Voices program was only on air for one hour, it was an hour to promulgate what was invisible within the mainstream media. I eagerly attended the Indigenous Broadcasters Conferences and found them stimulating, bringing back a mountain of visions only to have them shelved due to funding restraints.

All in all, I had been on the air for six years and loved promoting our Aboriginal music and our artists. Music was the rhythm of the soul and I reflected on its importance at our family gatherings. It took me years to understand its relationship to drinking, but I observed as I wept with my cousins. Music brought back memories for them. Memories made them sad. The more memories, the sadder they became, and the more they drank. Presenting an Indigenous radio program gave me a sensitivity to our music, the history behind it, and also the singers. It was an honour and a privilege and one of the great periods in my life.

In time Ron and I were fortunate enough to meet most of the singers and their bands. Music was a great healer so we organised socials and charity concerts. Each singer enriched our lives and left something with us. Mr Jimmy Little stayed with us in 1994, and he was the most gentle, humble and wise Aboriginal man I had ever met. I was thrilled to learn that his lovely wife Marge actually grew up in Coonamble with my mother. Aunty Marge shared many stories about Mum as a young schoolgirl. Uncle Jimmy was a household name, having been in the entertainment industry for many decades, and was greatly respected as a man who was so gentle and kind. Even though Uncle Jimmy was tired from doing a concert one Thursday night at a local shopping plaza, he was gracious enough to make a special effort to sit up with our son Tim until 1.00 am giving him advice and motivation to continue pursuing his interest with playing the guitar. In 1994 Uncle Jimmy recorded the song that he was born to sing. He was from Cummergunga Mission and his tribe was the Yorta Yorta, so he called his song 'Yorta Yorta Man'. It ends with the promising, haunting whispers of, 'Some day I know I will be returning like the legend of my tribal boomerang.'

To me this precious ambassader was a true elder and I loved, respected and recognised him as such. There had only been two other men that I recognised and respected as elders in the knowledge: Bob Randall and Bill Reid. Uncle Bob Randall was a singer/songwriter, counsellor, politician, Aboriginal teacher and consultant. Uncle Bob was from the

Arunta tribe in Alice Springs and had been taken from his parents as a baby boy. He grew up in the city, had a university education and was one of the radicals who fought for better and fairer conditions for all of us who live on today. He was a talented musician who left us with one of our most beloved songs about the stolen generations, 'My Brown Skinned Baby They Take Him Away'. Uncle Bob wasn't as fortunate as I was, because he never met his natural mother again. When he eventually retraced her and went back home he was crushed to find she had passed away six months previously, the same time he had written this inspiring song in which the last verse lamented, 'Upon this earth they never met again.'

The other elder was Uncle Bill Reid from Pilliga Scrub. He was not my blood relation but everyone called him Uncle as a sign of respect. He was dearly loved and accepted by both the black and white communities. The first time I interviewed this quietly spoken gentleman I was ecstatic to learn that he and my grandfather had grown up in the same era at Pilliga. He knew all my aunts and he spoke fondly of my mother Beatrice; he told me she had the best voice he had ever heard. I had a special place in my heart for someone who had been so close to my grandfather. These were two very proud and dignified men from the Gamilaroi tribe.

Uncle Bill lectured at TAFE. He was also a gifted artist who carved portraits of people on emu eggs. He would then thread minute wires through the eggs and transform them into lights. Uncle Bill was a knowledgeable historian and spent the best part of his life involved in reconciliation before the government made a policy of it. His passing was an enormous shock not only for his family but for everyone who came from the Gamilaroi tribe. We laid him to rest in Bourke in 1993 but his spirit as well as his children live on.

The radio program opened up many doors for me. On one hand it enabled me to meet our great artists and on the other it opened the doors to the community, and the grass roots people accepted me as they were familiar with my name from radio. This was an advantage for my role as the Community Development Officer.

YOUR PEOPLE WILL BE MY PEOPLE

After doing my Aboriginal studies I was troubled about having married a non-Aboriginal man when I was young and none the wiser, so when Uncle Bob Randall stayed with us, I asked him, 'Have I done the wrong thing by intermarrying?' In his caring way Uncle Bob replied, 'Donna, love is invisible. It doesn't have a colour.' This freed me from my guilt and enabled me to love unconditionally.

Ron had already proved himself. He was loving, faithful and understanding. He was a family man who never went 'out with the boys', and was a great provider. He was also a workaholic who had much job satisfaction as he was a first-class machinist and a perfectionist; nothing less was acceptable to him. At the dockyards, Ron was highly skilled; he worked the largest vertical borer in the southern hemisphere and the equipment from some of the break-down jobs he had to repair was so enormous it was unbelievable. After becoming a tradesperson he was made a leading hand in 1976, then promoted to foreman in 1979 and then appointed as an estimator in the final year. When the dockyard closed down Ron gained employment at Newcastle Engineering in 1986 and went back onto the machines he loved.

There were numerous occasions at work where he took a stand for Aboriginal people. It didn't enter the other workers' minds that Ron might be married to an Aboriginal woman, so whenever discussions came up and they voiced their opinions Ron took the opportunity to address their issues and promote some positive information. In so doing he lost a few friends he thought were mates, but on the whole he had a positive influence. He became skilled in dealing with racism and prejudice in the workplace and in many ways educated the workers around him. It wasn't easy being singled out at work but Ron took his stand and was respected for it.

My husband accepted my people as they were and would never treat them in a patronising way. My people were very perceptive and loved and accepted Ron because they knew he was sincere and genuine. Ron loved them before I fell in love with them, and I often thought about that Bible verse I'd read to him on our wedding night that went, 'And your people will be my people.'

PROMOTING OUR PEOPLE

The two-and-a-half-years I spent at college had paid off as I was using all the knowledge and research skills I learned there in my new job. I had several roles that I had to carry out within any given week. Work was challenging but I thrived on it: it gave me confidence and enhanced my cultural identity. The aim of the Awabakal Co-op was to provide services for the Aboriginal community, provide employment for the local Aboriginal people, and empower the local Aboriginal community. Having just emerged from my own identity crisis I had a sincere sensitivity for those going through the same search through similar circumstances. Being a resource information officer entailed forwarding information to students who wrote to the cultural centre requesting information for assignments they had on Aboriginal Australia. These were informative years for me as I became familiar with the local history about the

Awabakal tribe and the numerous family groups which were relocated in Newcastle.

I was also the Centre's part-time librarian and was responsible for a small collection which was loaned out. Whenever I had a spare moment I would read the books in the library which were all written by Aboriginal people from all over Australia. I particularly enjoyed the poetry books and the autobiographies. As I had written every assignment at college from an Indigenous perspective, I was familiar with many proficient writers and took the opportunity to read their books cover to cover.

I was also asked to be a guest speaker at numerous schools, churches, and community organisations such as Probus, Rotary, View and professional businesswomen's clubs. These speaking engagements increased my confidence and at the same time I was promoting the Awabakal Co-op.

Invitation followed invitation and soon I began part-time lecturing at five local TAFE colleges. TAFE introduced a new course called Career Education for Women (CEW) in 1990. It was an opportunity for women to learn about Aboriginal Australia and Koori women in society today. I loved promoting my people, educating non-Aboriginal people about our history, perspectives and the welfare state. The feedback assured me that I was able to influence many women in challenging their own belief systems and gave me confidence and hope to accept all speaking invitations. I only viewed myself as a guest speaker but I was paid at a lecturer's rate. In the six years of my employment I was asked to speak to over six hundred community groups. I found that I had a gift for talking to groups. I often marvelled why it was so easy when I remembered there was a time when I had great difficulty just saying hello to a stranger. The two largest audiences I had to address were three hundred first-year nursing students, and the Lord Mayor's prayer breakfast in 1994, which was attended by 1,600 people. My speaking engagements along with the two radio programs gave me great exposure, and I trust it helped change some opinions that society had about us.

My motivation for speaking had a very distinct origin. I recall how one night I got very angry with some ignorant comments that were reported on a TV program. It caused me great stress and three hours later, after giving it great consideration, I thought, If white society legitimately doesn't know about the consequences of government policies, then someone has to inform them. And so I accepted the challenges and began guest speaking. At times I was called away from home three nights a week until after a couple of years I paced myself, trying to keep work and home duties balanced.

Clare Saggus was the Regional Aboriginal Community Liaison Officer at the Department of School Education. She approached me one day and said, 'Donna, next week is Anzac Day, why don't you do a radio program on the Aboriginal Anzacs?' Clare told me how her uncle had served in World War II and after the war returned to Wilcannia without any recognition, medals or even a veteran's pension. Not only that, but he wasn't permitted to enter the RSL to have a drink with the other returned soldiers.

I hit the textbooks for ten hours and put together a program called 'Lest We Forget the Black Diggers', taking its title from a book of the same name. I was astounded to learn that over four thousand Aboriginal men in Queensland alone had enlisted in the armed services. I read out material from a few sources which documented our concentrated effort and involvement in World War I, World War II and the Vietnam War. I cried when I read that over sixty Aboriginal and Torres Strait Islanders were sent to Gallipoli: I was never taught this at school or at college.

Clare was so passionate about the discrimination that she suggested we march on Anzac Day in remembrance of our Indigenous servicemen. We encouraged another fifteen Koories to march with us in 1990. We were very nervous as we set off from the top of town as we didn't know what reception we would get from the white community. We were the last group to march and the response from the crowd was overwhelming. We had two elders, Mr Jack and Mrs June Thorpe, carry our banner emblazoned with the words 'Lest We Forget the Black Diggers'. It was a proud moment for us as now we could represent our fore-fathers who had fought for a land they had already lost. We walked the streets knowing they were the forgotten heroes. We felt honoured to represent them and also knew that by our presence we would stimulate conversations and promote knowledge about Indigenous involvement in the wars.

The next year we had the coordinator of the Awabakal Elders Service head our march and we felt so proud as he was a returned soldier from Vietnam. Dave Nean had never marched and so we felt honoured that now he joined us. He was surprised at the respect and response from white society, so surprised that, as he marched, he couldn't hold back the tears. This was what my work was all about: bring-ing awareness through community education and using everyday situations to highlight our involvement and achievements. And promoting our people at their best was what I enjoyed doing most.

I held art exhibitions promoting what our brothers were doing whilst serving their time in prison. I set up a support group for Aboriginal women who were going through bereavement and set up the Elders Meal Day which was held once a fortnight and enabled the elders to socialise and interact with each other. Arranging socials taught me many organisational skills and provided the opportunity for Ron and myself to show our commitment to the local Aboriginal community. One year we had planned the staff Christmas party and had booked three Aboriginal groups to sing. They were Roz Webb from Sydney, Col Hardy and his band from Sydney, as well as Roger Knox from Tamworth.

As the date drew closer I was asking around the community if we had anyone who could play piano. June Thorpe told me Ray Kelly had a brother in Sydney who was magic with a piano. We tracked him down and found out the nuns were looking after him and I asked if they would be able to drive him up to Newcastle to play at the social. It was a big ask. Our brother had lost his way due to alcohol but the nuns said that the opportunity would be really wonderful for him, and that they would try to convince him to make the trip.

No-one expected the heatwave we had to endure on that day so keeping our brother away from the hotel was more than a challenge for the nuns. However, they excelled. At eight that evening I introduced Frankie Franklin and there was a drum roll as he walked on stage. The whole auditorium went silent as we watched our very own black Liberace perform. He sat tall and proud on that mulga wood piano seat. He had amazing rhythm and played by ear. His fingers danced along the black and white keyboard, his delight evident at being back in the spotlight. There wasn't a dry eye in the house. That gave me so much joy. To take someone who was in the gutter and place him on stage to remind him how special he was. That was what I wanted to do for my people.

The highlights of my job were too numerous to mention. I spent six wonderful years working amongst my people. Promoting them through broadcasting, coordinating the resource centre, producing quarterly newsletters, and working with the elders, all enabled me to learn more from their life experiences and more about our evolving Aboriginal culture.

WALKABOUT

There is, however, one episode that will remain with me as long as I live. I had only been employed for four months when I was invited to go walkabout with the Culture Officer, Paul Gordon. Paul had arranged a busload of non-Aboriginal people to spend a week at Brewarrina and Bourke, looking at sites, learning about Aboriginal culture and living out under the stars.

On the third night our camps were flooded with torrential rain which lasted for an entire week. During daylight we had to leave the campsite and walk to the nearest cover, a sheep shed about eleven kilometres away. The heavens just opened up and we had to walk in the pouring rain as there were no trees to provide shelter. The red dirt had turned to slimy red butter. Each time we pulled our feet up from the mud, there were almost ten centimetres of mud attached to the soles. It was like walking on the moon.

The walk was slow and tiring. We had at least five people on the walk who were over fifty years of age and I was concerned about their health. By the end of the first day's walk-out the bus, four-wheel drive and trailer were all bogged and we were stranded. As we continued the eighteen-kilometre walk-out the next day I realised why our people travelled light, only taking what they needed for each day. Paul gave directions to take the tourists to his mother's house on the Brewarrina Mission as she would gladly put us up. Paul decided to stay in the sheep shed until the rain stopped and then try to free the bogged vehicles. During the six-hour walk I reminded myself that it was three years to the day that we had laid Beatrice to rest and here I was trying to survive in the bush on a walkabout.

When we arrived on the mission, Mrs Gordon welcomed us into her home. She didn't question having seventeen extra people sleeping over for a couple of days. As I slept on the lounge that night I tried to imagine, if it were in reverse in the city, what reception we would have had. I wondered if a white family really would welcome seventeen Aboriginal strangers into their home, open up their cupboards and say, 'Eat all you want.'

That night all of the group wanted to head into town to celebrate their survival. They headed for the hotel. I saw a group of Koories talking out the front of the hotel so I decided to go and befriend them, and found they were familiar with my name from radio. We sat on the cement footpath and they freely talked with me for over an hour. I asked them questions about race relations, police attitudes, black deaths in custody, land rights, unemployment, education, youth, women, substance abuse, housing and the Aboriginal history of Bre. I was fascinated. My only regret was that I didn't have a tape recorder going. To my surprise even though the people were drinking, they knew all the answers and freely disclosed information. I had to go to college for two-and-a-half years to learn what they already knew. But I was grieved as I realised these people knew the answers but were powerless to make any changes.

We had only been given the right to vote in 1967 – up until then we were not consulted for any decisions and we were not permitted to have a voice. The government administered the Assimiliation Policy from 1936 to 1965. Their aim was to take more control over Aboriginal people and force them to learn the new white ways. Under this policy the government had the powers to remove Aboriginal children from their natural families. This was a direct attempt to eradicate Aboriginal culture. Inland children were transported to the coast and coastal children were taken inland, placed into homes and not permitted to contact their relations until they turned fifteen. Over 5,600 Aboriginal children were forcefully removed and brought to live in the city to learn the white ways. That is why my siblings and I were sent away that day in Coonamble. This policy took effect all over Australia and now all over Australia Aboriginal people are still trying to find their way back home to their people.

These people in Bre remembered when in the late sixties there was segregation at the swimming pools, theatres and schools. Our men who worked on cattle stations only received equal wages in 1984. Although I knew these facts from a textbook it was much more convincing listening to people who had experienced it and lived to tell it.

Our people in this group gave me a special gift that day. They had just proved to me that even though they were drinkers, they were also taxpayers and community citizens who had the right to voice their opinion, plus they had something important to say. I gave each one of them a kiss and they kissed me goodbye. I was glad they accepted me and my heart went out to them as they said, 'Thank you for talking to us. Everyone in this town calls us drunks. No-one talks to us.' Up until that day I'd had a fear of anyone who drank, but from that time on I wasn't afraid or ashamed to talk to them.

FINDING A LIFETIME

Over the next couple of years my Aboriginal family came to Newcastle and delighted us with their presence. This included my sisters and brothers, Tom, Jayne, Darlie, Sooty, Barry, Robby, Aunty Ivy, Aunty Tam and cousins Bronco, Pat, Kelly, Tibby, Rosie and Doll-Doll. I felt special being their host.

These were happy times, always emotional but incredibly special. Here we were brothers, sisters and cousins trying to get to know one another, trying to catch up on a lifetime in a weekend or sometimes a week. Society just takes for granted spending Christmas or celebrating your birthday together with your brothers and sisters, but for us we didn't have that privilege. We missed out on natural family disputes and sibling rivalry so coming together as adults was an unusual experience.

Barry's first visit is as vivid today as it was then. Ron

answered the front door, but left Barry standing there as he thought he was a door-to-door salesman. It had been six years since we'd last seen Barry and Ron didn't recognise him as he stood waiting to be asked in. Barry had lost lots of weight since Kim's twenty-first and had gone fairly bald on top, so he had to introduce himself to Ron. We had lots of fun for the seven days he was with us. We usually went to bed at eleven o'clock but while Barry was visiting we would sit up talking until after one o'clock, sharing what little memories we had at the camp, the childhood that followed our early years, and our lives in the city with our families.

Barry had commenced the Adult Aboriginal Studies Course at Tranby Aboriginal College in Sydney in 1990, and would come on his way to Sydney for block placements four times per year. Barry, Wendy and his children Jeffrey, Belinda, Denise and little Barry were living in Bourke and this was too far for us to travel out to visit them, so he was a special guest when he came to our place. Tim was thirteen when Barry came for his first visit and it was during this time that he showed Tim how to play a few chords on a guitar, stimulating an undiscovered talent in our second son. This was the greatest thing that Tim learned from Barry.

Barry was a natural born entertainer and so every night I invited people over to our house to meet him and I would ask him to sing for us. I loved his singing and thought he sang songs better than his favourite singer, Charlie Pride. One particular song was his favourite, 'So Afraid of Losing You Again', and as I had never heard it before it will always remind me of our first time together as adults.

I couldn't help but get emotional when he sang as it would always stir feelings about Grandfather and our mother. I felt stupid crying, but Barry told me that all the Welshes were very emotional and that I was just like Aunty Joan and Aunty Audrey who would always end up crying after a round of songs. By the end of the visit both Ron and I were physically and mentally drained. It took so much energy concentrating on the topics Barry discussed. He couldn't stay focused on one subject and moved from one conversation to another, and then after ten minutes he would bring you back to the original topic. This was coupled by the emotional aspect of being reunited with my brother. Going from an extreme high, crying from laughter, to an extreme low, weeping from sorrow. Every visit was like this. A weekend emotional roller-coaster ride. Trying to catch up on thirty years in one week or weekend. He needed to make people happy and to laugh as it covered up the pain he secretly hid deep within. When he sang and I cried it was because the emotion he sang with came from down deep in his soul.

He took his role as big brother seriously as he felt obliged to help, to offer advice to all of us, and to visit regularly to make sure we were getting on with our lives. He wanted to meet Mum so we all went shopping together. At all times he called her 'Mum' out of respect and Mum thought it was wonderful. She said to him, 'I always wanted a son.' Barry often spoke about having a big Welsh family reunion. So I left it to him, being the eldest. Before he left to go home I recorded us speaking on cassette and I asked him, 'How have you enjoyed your week, our first time together since you were nine?'

He answered, 'I wouldn't have missed it for the world.'

Belonging

SORRY SIGHT

On Boxing Day 1989, we left Newcastle to go on holi-days at Lightning Ridge. We had friends from CB radio living there, working an opal mine. This was our first trip to the much-talked-about town of Lightning Ridge, plus my brother Sooty and his wife, Shirley, lived there. It was an unusually interesting place to live and we had the royal tour of the town as our friends John and Ingram showed us the importance of the town's survival upon the opal. John explained the way of life and the numerous people that helped to bring colour to the town. We stood amazed as we looked at the multi-millionaires who were dressed in the most casual clothes. They lived in improvised tin huts as transporting bricks and timber to the Ridge was far too costly. It was a real education for both Ron, myself and our young boys. If John hadn't taken us around and explained everything, I would have only seen the mounds of dirt and missed out on understanding the culture of the town.

It was the peak of their summer and at night it seemed the whole town met at the bore baths. This was an underground hot water spring, and many tourists came to see the opals as well as visit the hot springs. As I played with Mark, I listened to the various conversations people held sitting around the edge of the pool. Business deals were struck, employment opportunities, coordination of ideas, investments, as well as the usual pool-side gossip. It was an enlightening place and for me it seemed there was a workable equality as I watched young and old, black and white, male and female, rich and poor, all sitting in swimmers at the edge of the pool trying to find relief from the heat of the day. There was such a mixture of races it could have been the league of nations. I saw multiculturalism at work and this was perhaps one of the facinating aspects which made us appreciate the town: there was not only the wealth of its sacred stone but a great value that was placed on human lives. I spoke with many Aboriginal people who were all contented living at the Ridge and who said they felt accepted by the mainstream society. There was no hint of racism, and the Ridge was a magical place where everyone lived in hope of finding the next big strike.

We had only been there three days when we heard that an earthquake had hit Newcastle. Ron couldn't relax and felt guilty being on holidays when we heard reports of such devastation, and so he decided to head back home and help with the recovery. We spent the last night with Sooty and Shirley and, as always, spent most of the night browsing through the collection of photographs and conversing over them. Over the years I had learned that houses were for sleeping in, cars for transport, no matter how old, rough or what model. Regardless how many people piled into a car, seatbelts were not used. As Koories had few material items to hoard, their family photos, past and present, were their prized possessions. Many people I visited, it was common knowledge that when they knew their family members were coming for a stay over, they would hide their photos and even lock them in a room so as to ensure their safety.

One meal and a few short treasured hours were all I had to spend with my brother and his family, but we hoped to return to once again inhale the uniqueness of this place where people lived for their dreams.

We called into Coonamble cemetery on the way back, to see Beatrice's resting place. We knew it had a small white cross at the foot of the grave to identify it, but the cross was not visible so we walked up and down the rows trying to find it. When we found the grave, there was no cross to distinguish it, only a small, rugged broken-brown piece of fence paling with the words quickly scratched on, 'B. Welsh'. It was shameful. Our hearts sank as we weren't expecting such a sorry sight. Ron got all choked up and as he blew his nose he said, 'We've got to do something about that, buy a headstone, even if I have to pay for it myself. That's disgusting. She deserves better. She did so much for Coonamble.'

BEATRICE WELSH MEMORIAL DAY

Five years after we buried my mother, we held the Beatrice Welsh Memorial Day. I made posters with her photograph in the middle and displayed these all down the main street of Coonamble in shop windows, on billboards, telegraph poles and phone booths. These marked the streets reminding people that this was her day. I didn't want people to forget her name and so we arranged a dance for 8 May 1991. We booked Roger Knox and Euraba, a Koori band from Tamworth, accompanied by Tracey Lee Gray from Coonabarabran, to sing at the dance. I met a lot of the women down the street earlier through the day as they did their Saturday shopping and each one commented how they were excited about the dance, and looking forward to getting dressed up for a night out. The only time they got dressed up was for a funeral and so I was pleased that they were filled with anticipation.

I made the hall as pretty as I could by placing lilac streamers around the room and on the stage, plus a spray of lilac flowers on each table. I chose this colour as it was Bea's favourite and I wanted everything to help people remember her. I had a decorated cake ordered and the iced flowers were made in lilac and purple. Eleven glasses were presented to each of Beatrice's children. The glasses had the logo I designed inscribed on the side as well as our Christian names. These were inscribed in gold and were to be highly valued by each of us. My sister Kim suggested we also present young Jamie with a glass. Although he was Mum's grandson, she raised him and he was so close to his Nana. I agreed with my sister, and to see Jamie's face as he held his glass made it all worth while.

It was a lovely night and I was so impressed with the respect the crowd showed for my mother. All night long different people would come up to Ron and me and share their fondest memories of my mother. The eldest son, Barry, as well as Uncle Cyril, Aunty Audrey, Aunty Joan and Aunty Tam, all gave speeches, plus the local auditor, Mr Beade Waterford, who had known Beatrice even before her children were removed from her care.

They all gave a wonderful testimony. We then had a one-minute silence and everyone was upstanding. This was followed by a tape with Mum singing 'How Great Thou Art'. As we listened to her voice the room was full of Aboriginal people who had their heads bowed and their eyes full of tears. 'Nugget', the local reporter, came and gave us a wonderful two-page coverage and it was good to see a positive report in the local newspaper.

The local police approached us, astonished that there wasn't a hint of trouble. No fights. No breakages. And what they couldn't believe was that there was no-one in the street after the dance. Apparently when the pubs close, people tend to hang around and sit in the main street, but on this occasion everyone went directly home and within thirty minutes there wasn't a sign of anybody in the main street or on any street in the whole town. Ron told the officer, 'Well, they had a good night, they've gone home. They had a Koori band so why not allow Aboriginal people to organise a night that they can enjoy and then they can go home satisfied and happy.'

The policeman said again, 'This is the first time they've gone straight home.' I was glad that we had broken a couple of barriers down – that's what I was called to do, to be a peacemaker.

The dance raised $1,000, which went towards the band and the beautiful headstone we had transported out west from Newcastle. We had inscribed in gold the words:

> Her life was not measured in the years she lived
> But in the love that she gave us all.

This seemed to capture Beatrice and the meaning of her life as well as what she meant to others.

WASTED YEARS

I n the following years I obtained so much information
about my natural mother. Seems like what Ron and I
knew was only the surface and we both got excited each
time we learned something new about her. Barry told me
she had won thirteen talent quests straight. Col Hardy (an
Aboriginal singer) told me how Mum had beaten him in
the Walgett Talent Quest. He said, 'Oh Beatie was lovely.
I owe her a lot. She should be on stage, not me.' Different
aunts told me she sang on ABC Radio in one of those radio
serials, 'Days with Hector', and also how she was asked to
sing before the Queen in Sydney in 1977, but she'd said she
couldn't leave her children in Coonamble. She was known
as the 'Black Connie Francis' or the 'Black Patsy Cline'.

In order to keep her memory alive, Ron and I donated
a trophy four years in a row to the Tamworth Country
Music Festival. We wanted white society to know about

her and we didn't want black society to forget her. The trophy was also to inspire Aboriginal people to get up and sing. The winners have been:

1991   Buddy Knox from Tamworth
1992   Gnarnayarrahe Waitairie from Brisbane
1993   John Turner from Mt Isa
1994   Kim and Trish Freeman from Inverell
1995   Moree Koori Kids.

Kim made it to the Tamworth Music festival in 1992 to present the trophy and after being there and seeing the look on the winner's face, she understood why it was so important to us. This was something little we could do to try and make up for the wasted years when we didn't know her. The trophy had the power to encourage people to keep on trying.

After the presentation in 1994, a man in the audience came backstage to see me. It was my natural father, Morrie. He had made it over from Wee Waa with a busload of Aboriginal elders who'd come to see the award. I was thrilled that Morrie was there to see what we were doing for Bea's memory. He was pleased. He stood silently looking at the trophy and I knew his heart was filled with memories. No-one knew her voice better and no-one was missing it as much as dear Morrie. He eventually started a new life and now had a lovely lady called Peggy looking after him in that quiet little place called Wee Waa.

The motivation behind my studies and my work was the guilt I carried for so long and I knew I threw every ounce of energy into my work as I was trying to make up to my people for twenty-seven years when I lived in denial, when I didn't identify. For me work is spiritual. A feeling to give. A feeling to be accepted. A feeling of weeping, to weep with my people and to laugh with them. A feeling of sharing. To share with my people what I have learned so they too can be empowered. Gradually I am making up for all the wasted years and with each year my wounded heart is healing too.

After Bea passed away, Aunty Ivy started to visit during the school holidays. It was strange not having an aunty when I was growing up, and now I was getting to know my aunt when she was in her seventies. She often remarked, 'When I look at you I see Beadie,' but I would say, 'When I look at you, you remind me of her.'

Aunty Ivy loved coming down for a rest. It was a break from Walgett. She loved walking around the lake at sunset and looking at all the colourful gardens and the pretty traffic lights. We would visit Aboriginal families as well as go to church. On Saturday we would visit Mum and go shopping. Every time we drove away from Mum's house, Aunty would say, 'What a beautiful person she is. I thank God He sent you to them. It's so wonderful how He knew everything and worked it out.'

It was on such an afternoon that Aunty mentioned staying with some lovely white people in their house at Shortland. She said that in her younger years she and her daughter Judy would travel around attending church rallies. She asked me where Sandgate was. I told her that was my church and that it was where Ron and I had married. Aunt said she stayed with the Nicholses. I told her how I knew them and how lovely they were to me and how Daph had prepared the flowers in the church for our wedding day. The Nicholses never knew that Aunt's maiden name was Welsh, as they referred to her as Ivy Kennedy from Walgett – and all that time the Nicholses were praying for her niece, watching me growing up.

Out of all the Baptist churches in Australia why did God choose to send Aunty Ivy to Sandgate Baptist? Because He knew I was there. I remember a chorus I learned as a teenager that went:

> In His time, in His time
> He makes everything so beautiful
> In His time.

And another one:

> Something beautiful, something good
> All my confusion, He understood
> All I had to offer Him
> Was brokenness and strife
> But He made something beautiful of my life.

FAMILY REUNION

Four months after the memorial day and dance, our family was grieved to hear that Uncle Cyril had died from a heart attack. Unbelievably, only fifteen months later, my dearly beloved Aunty Margaret suddenly passed away, on Boxing Day 1993. We laid her next to her loving husband. The two relations I first made contact with and who put me in contact with my birth mother were now both gone.

In July 1994 Barry decided to spend the weekend with us and came up from his studies in Sydney after his last lecture on Friday. Three hours later, Kim and Jayne walked through the door. Jayne had come from Cairns and called into Kim's at Gunnedah and they'd decided to come to Newcastle for a few days. I was surprised that they all arrived on the same weekend without contacting each other.

Jayne wanted to find her twin brother and so picked up from the last clues we had of Wayne living in Newcastle. I suggested Jayne try the electoral roll first and see if he may be in Newcastle but I wasn't confident, it was just a starting point. On Monday morning I went to work at the youth centre and gave my sisters directions to get into the city. Upstairs at the youth centre we had a TAFE outreach course running, and I arranged for Barry to go and speak to the students for an hour, talking about his life in Bourke and his studies in Sydney. One hour later the girls returned and I thought they must have got lost. Both Jayne and Kim had miserable-looking faces and I knew they hadn't found out anything.

On the contrary, they had traced our baby brother Wayne back to an address in Newcastle, not far from where I was working. We'd both been in the same town for two decades and never knew. It was cause for great celebration. We wondered how many times we might have passed one another on the street not knowing we were brother and sister. That night Wayne, his wife Robyn, and their two children, Blane and Ryianna, came to meet us. There was no doubt it was him as the twins looked alike and Ryianna could have been Jayne's little girl, she was such the image of her.

As I come to the final chapters it is with a heavy heart that I report that we laid my dear brother Barry Butt to rest in March 1994. With his passing came the determination to uphold the promise I made to him when we first met in 1984. Barry wanted a complete new start to his life and moved his family to Riverview in Queensland, in early January. Just six weeks later he was taken by a severe heart attack. Poor Kim had all the responsibility of arranging the funeral from Riverview. Kim, Debbie, Sonny and their families had also moved to Riverview in January, to make a new life and in better hope for employment, but now they were feeling isolated.

Our family normally used the largest church in Coonamble for our funerals as we had such large ones, but this time we couldn't get access because the minister would be away on a conference. I asked him if one of the deacons could come and open up the church but we were denied again: he was adamant that we might 'run amok, and then who would be responsible?' So I obtained permission to use the Uniting Church. Their minister said he was unable to do the service as it was his day off, so I was very appreciative when the minister from my church in Newcastle agreed to travel out west on his day off and take the service. Pastor Dennis and Elaine Carter showed by their love how they were prepared to 'go the extra mile'.

When we entered the church early Monday morning to set up the chairs, one of the church elders greeted us warmly and said, 'We stopped the Aboriginal people coming here fifteen years ago but today we open up the doors, welcome them back and ask their forgiveness.' As I sat inside the church I couldn't help but think, That's another barrier we broke down.

I invited the elder to come to the funeral as I wanted him to see Aboriginal people at a funeral. Aboriginal people are always so respectful at funerals, it's part of our culture. It's very important to say 'Goodbye'. It's important to go back to the land of your borning – that's why Aboriginal people want to go back home to be buried and not be buried in the city. It's important to know your relationship to each other and your relationship to the land.

Close to three hundred friends and relatives farewelled my brother. Kim, Debbie, Sonny and Darlie all came down from Riverview in Queensland. Sooty came from Lightning Ridge and Jayne travelled all the way from Cairns by train. Widdy and Robby were already living in Coonamble. It was the first time Jayne and Wayne were together in their home town since they were kids. Spending time with the cousins and the family was the beginning of healing for Wayne.

Pastor Dennis Carter was very sensitive and spoke with compassion at the service. I have attended enough funerals for Aboriginal people and at virtually every funeral I've listened to ministers who couldn't help themselves and have come on real heavy instead of focusing with sensitivity upon the bereaved. Dennis and Elaine had been missionaries in the Philippines and knew what it was like to be the only white people among the crowd. They understood what it was like to be the minority within the dominant society. Plus they were both filled with love for people and showed respect and sensitivity for another culture. In closing the service, Pastor Dennis said, 'It was Barry's dream to have a family reunion, to have all of his brothers and sisters together at once. Today his dream came true.'

Elaine was surprised to see the police escort the funeral through the town. We drove two abreast from the church to the cemetery which completely stopped all the traffic as we took Barry on his last drive through his beloved town. Four police officers marked the corners of the main intersection of Coonamble and as the coffin passed by them, each saluted. One of my brothers travelled in Elaine and Dennis' vehicle and Elaine commented, 'Isn't that lovely how they show respect?' My brother, crying, replied, 'They respect us in death, why can't they respect us in life?'

COMING TOGETHER DAY

Working at Awabakal Co-op gave me significant experience, not just learning from my people, but also meeting many sincere and caring non-Aboriginal people. I first heard of the Newcastle Aboriginal Support Group back in 1986 during my university studies and when I commenced employment at Awabakal in December 1988, I realised then the commitment and involvement of the Support Group. Jim Wright, administrator of the co-op, delegated the Support Group's *Coming Together Day* project to me when I was still the Community Development and Resource Officer. It was my role to promote the idea within the Aboriginal community and to ascertain whether or not local Koories wanted to 'come together'. People listened, but made no comment. Did they want to participate? I was uncertain.

There were numerous meetings with Moya Farrell and Lorraine Robertson on how we would organise the day.

We invited Dave Nean, who was the coordinator of the Awabakal Elders Service, to bring the elders to the event so that non-Aboriginal people attending could be presented to them. There would be a few speeches which would clarify the aims and objectives of the gathering. We would also ask participants to sign a commitment. This was a wonderfully worded document, something like a mini-treaty. It wasn't about owning guilt of the past. It was about owning responsibility for the future.

The day was a hot, humid Sunday and we planned to meet at 2.00 pm on the foreshore. I had a twenty-minute drive into town and while I drove I felt a bit awkward, as I thought maybe fifty people would turn up. I had offered to transport others but no-one had responded. I thought that surely there must be at least ten other Aboriginal people who believed in reconciliation.

But, as I drove along the foreshore, I could see a large gathering. I was thrilled. They had come. My heart beat faster and my eyes filled with tears as the huge number of people became evident. It restored my faith in humanity, that there were indeed conscientious people who acknowledged the past and who wanted to be reconciled to the future of this country. As I walked past those smiling faces waiting to be received by the elders, I felt something special was happening. Over one-and-a-half thousand white people lined the foreshore. It was the making of history. It was a sacred meeting.

I spotted a very dark Aboriginal woman whom I had never seen before. I introduced myself and found out her name was Rosie and that she came from the Northern Territory. Although she had been drinking earlier, I invited her to sit with the elders to meet with the people. I stood back and observed the pride that welled up within her while she was representing her people and seeing the white people responding to her with respect. The white people were glad to meet her. Most shook hands but many greeted her with a kiss. After about twenty minutes of greeting people, she left her seat and went back to the hill. When I enquired why she had left, she told me: 'Sister, I bin drinking. I embarrassed.' She refused to return, even after I tried to convince her that her breath didn't matter and that we were honoured by her presence. She said: 'Thank you for asking me. Being down there was very special. I won't forget this day.'

The Awabakal elders were tired after shaking hands for over an hour-and-a-half. Their participation was not only in keeping with Aboriginal protocol. It was also significant on both a personal and spiritual level. One sixty-year-old white lady came up to me with tears rolling down her cheeks. She held my hand, and said: 'I was one of them. I took the children away from their parents. I am sorry. I thought we were doing the right thing. Today is the first time I have told anyone. I'm so sorry.'

I kissed her. I was one of those children who was taken away. She didn't need to know that. I wasn't angry. My heart was filled with love. I hugged her and said, 'Thank you for coming.'

Yes, the day was a historical event for Newcastle. It was a success. It took courage to make a stand. The tears that fell bore evidence to the healing process that began on that humid afternoon. We will never know how many hearts were touched that day. We can only know that when people from diverse cultures come together, whatever our personal agendas may be, when we come with goodwill and courage, then we will connect, we will have a sacred encounter and spiritual healing will take place.

JUST WAIT

Paul Walsh had a vision to produce a book called *Novocastrian Tales*, to be launched in 1997, during the bicentenary year of Newcastle. He had asked close to forty authors, including myself, to contribute short stories and poetry. I submitted a story about reconciliation called 'The Coming Together Day'. Encouraged by Paul's positive feedback, I asked if he would care to read my autobiography. Upon reading it, Paul asked my permission to include 'Joy Ride' and 'Boomerang Words' in *Novocastrian Tales*.

I had entered my book in the Indigenous Writers' Competition twice to no avail. *Novocastrian Tales* was the springboard to place me in the writers' circle. The timing was perfect. In the political arena there was a Royal Commission into the removal of Aboriginal children from their families and 'Joy Ride' proved to be a very popular and emotive story. Late 1997, I was asked to record it for the

ABC to be played on Radio National during the Christmas break; however it was a few months before it went to air.

My New Year's resolution was to keep my promise to my brother, complete the project and see the book published. By mid-February, early one Saturday morning, I had completed the fourth and what I thought was the final draft. I hesitated, closed the folder slowly and contentedly said, 'Lord, it's finished. What should I do now?' The silence was stunning and from within it He whispered, 'Just wait.' Throughout that week I wondered if I had heard correctly. I thought of sending copies off to publishers but my heart kept echoing, 'just wait'.

On the following Friday I arrived home from a media release at John Hunter Hospital, where Paul Walsh and his partner Suzanne Harvey had announced that the total sales from the book *Novocastrian Tales* had raised all the funds needed to build the Aboriginal Accommodation Centre at the hospital, and also enough for half the furniture. We, the Aboriginal community, will never be able to say thank you enough to Paul and Suzanne, these special people, who cared enough and went about advocating and negotiating to ensure that this much-needed accommodation was built, from the bottom up. One man's vision was adopted and shared by the wider community, and the action out of it was reconciliation.

I had only been at home for ten minutes and was heading towards the back door on a business trip to Sydney, when the phone rang. I told my husband, 'If it's for me tell them I'm not home.' Ron insisted I take the call after he answered it. It was Suzanne and Paul, and after a brief conversation I left for Sydney.

The story 'Joy Ride' went to air on ABC Radio National

about midday that day, and a lady in Canberra, who was driving in her car, heard it and was so intrigued she pulled off to the side of the road to listen to it. Nine-thirty that night I had a life-changing phone call from that lady. Her name was Carmel Bird, an author with many novels to her credit. We spoke for half an hour. She wanted to include 'Joy Ride' in her latest book *The Stolen Children – Their Stories*. There was an air of urgency as her book would be published within four weeks, but I agreed.

We chatted as if we were long-lost friends. I told Carmel about asking what to do next and how I was told to 'just wait'. She said that this could be the answer, as she normally never drives during the day, but she had to pay her car rego; also she never has the car radio on, but somehow it was and she heard my voice and was so interested that she had to stop and listen. To ease my curiosity I casually asked Carmel to tell me a little about Random House. I was staggered when she told me that it was big – a big multi-national publishing house. Carmel then asked me to send down my autobiography to her as she had connections and was sure they would be interested in it. Within a week I received a contract from Random House. I was told to wait and now I am standing where some writers yearn for years to be. I just seem to swing from star to star.

For our people who are still searching for their families I pray that you find the answers your heart needs to know. For the thousands who were institutionalised and unloved in your childhood and ignored and unwanted when you returned home, we weep with you. We need to hear your story. May you find the courage to walk forward and share your story. I pray you will find real love and healing.

I also hope this book is an encouragement to those

parents who have adopted children, to let them know that they can share a love as deep as the ocean. As I have shared my story at over six hundred meetings, many women have come up to me in tears because they have adopted children from overseas, and I could hear the despair in their voices. I tell them, 'I believe you have been called to be a channel of blessing. There are many reasons why a mother may have to give up her baby or child. Allow those special children to learn as much about both cultures. Give them many opportunities. Be open and honest. Immerse them in a sea of love.' And then I remind them of Uncle Bob's words when he said, 'Love doesn't have a colour.'

I will not deny the love of my parents who raised me. Just because they had white skin doesn't mean they didn't know how to love. I will not deny the strength I found through faith in God. I have met many wonderful Aboriginal Christians from all over Australia. Just because you call yourself a Christian doesn't mean you have to deny your Aboriginality.

A lot of water has gone under the bridge and a lot of that water came from my tears. Tears of the past, the loss, the unknown, the confusion, anger and sadness for the innocent victims – and recently, tears of happiness.

People probably think that just because we live in the city and eat the same foods as they do and speak the same language and dress the same way that I have assimilated. The difference is that to assimilate one has to conform to the values, beliefs, ethics, mores and accept the entrenched ideologies of the dominant culture. I have assumed a certain lifestyle but I breathe a living culture every day. I think of a black perspective all the time whether I am enjoying music, art, TV, conversation, dress or values. Perhaps my birth mother knew that she never really signed me away with the adoption papers as she knew that old Murri spirit will never let go of its own blood. That old Murri spirit will always call her children home.

That old Murri spirit is always there, day and night. When we lose our way, and the time is right, that old Murri spirit will call to us and we will hear the echoes of the past. Each time I meet someone who is on their journey home I just want to hold them and say, 'You are not alone, there are thousands of us back-tracking too.'

THE HEALING STRENGTH OF LOVE

I feel my life has been encircled by love. My mum in Newcastle is a special person. To me she is my mum — she raised me, taught me, cared for me and loved me. She taught me the real measure of love. She freed me. Love doesn't keep people captured. Love doesn't possess people. Real love means setting people free. She wept as much as I did when we found out that the government was behind the policy to separate children. We can't change what happened but I am very thankful that I was placed with a tender, loving family who loved enough to adopt, to commit themselves to loving, for a lifetime.

The love of my husband taught me to trust people and allow them to love me. He restored my faith in human nature. In 1993 Ron had an accident, leaving him with a permanent back injury which meant he would never again work the heavy machinery he loved so. This was a most difficult time in our marriage history, as I struggled to accept the injury, loss of security and the loss of a certain kind of lifestyle we had become accustomed to. Not that we were anywhere near being rich, but it's not until those things are abruptly removed that you realise the importance of independence. This difficult, imposed transition taught me to understand the depth of meaning in our wedding vows which say:

> For better for worse
> For richer for poorer
> In sickness and in health
> Until death do us part.

Unconditional love is for always. No matter what may come, no matter how long it will last, I will be there for you regardless.

During this transition time our second son, Tim, was diagnosed with a rare skull tumour. The specialist had only seen five of these particular tumours and impressed upon us the urgency to operate. If it had attached to the membranes of the brain it would affect Tim's memory and reflexes. Tim was a gifted musician and he would rather die than live without his guitar. The tumour had eaten two inches of his skull and with the urgent need to operate, the doctor had him admitted into hospital that day and scheduled the operation the next morning. Tim was operated on two days before he turned sixteen. I refused to buy a present for him that year. I told him he was given life for his sixteenth birthday, it was a miracle and not to be taken lightly. It was the surety of God's love, and the love of my mum, my husband and the love of friends that reinforced the power and healing strength of love which enabled me to breeze through yet another crisis.

Miracles happened at our house all the time and we were so thankful when the doctor reported six months later there were no signs of the tumour regrowing. Another miracle occurred when my eldest son, Darren, was given an opportunity to travel to America and work as a pit crew member for the American Racing Team in 1993.

It was always his dream to see the speedway circuits in the USA and it's a wonderful thing as a parent to see your children's dreams come true. He was forever the quiet achiever and we were thrilled that he had been given this fantastic opportunity. But letting go of my firstborn was the hardest thing I had ever had to do, as when he came into my life he meant the world to me and now I was setting him free to see the world for himself.

In January 1998 I took Tim, my twenty-year-old son, back to Coonamble for a week. During that time Widdy taught Tim how to carve emu eggs and since then Tim has carved six wonderful eggs. It was a spiritual trip in more ways than one. How inspiring it is to see your children searching for their roots and developing their own identity; to see that sacred trust being passed from one generation to another.

Mark is a mature nineteen-year-old who has completed his first year at TAFE in Automative and is also involved with the Speedway, just like Darren. He has a refreshing sense of humour and brings joy to all who know him.

I commenced employment with the Department of School Education in September 1994, situated in the District Office, but most of my work is out in the community. The vast majority of my workload at Awabakal Co-op was in community education so I feel as if I was unofficially employed by the Department for a number of years. My main role now within the Department is to support our Koori children and assist them to succeed despite the system. Knowledge is power. Education is the key to unlocking the poverty cycle. We need to educate the teachers so they have a strong understanding about Aboriginal history as misleading information is so damaging, and teachers have the power to influence the attitudes of thousands of children.

I am a dreamer. I dream of healing for our people. I dream of a time when our people will be recognised, respected and appreciated for the race they represent. I dream of justice instead of injustice and I dream of a better world for our children's children. My dream of having brothers and sisters came true. My dream of becoming a real Aboriginal, born in the spirit, came true. My dream of graduating came true. My dream of working for my people came true, and as long as I live I shall have a valley of beautiful dreams for my people.

I am still learning from my people. There is so much to know about Aboriginal history and the thing I love most is to watch our people communicating. I have been asked to share my story many times and am always emotional telling it, as I remember the places, the people, the heart. The hardest day in my life was National Sorry Day in 1998. I am sure that it was a day where a lot of awareness was raised, but for me it was heart rending. I had to speak at three different school assemblies and so driving to each location I was able to tune into the local talkback radio and hear the community's response to the observance day. The negative comments made me shudder as I realised how many people resisted the truth. I was glad my mum, Beatrice, was not here as it was all too painful.

That evening there was a special service at the cathedral to commemorate the Stolen Children. Sir Ronald Wilson from the Reconciliation Committee was the special guest. He had headed the enquiry into the removal of Aboriginal children from their families and presented the report, *Bringing Them Home*. Over five hundred people attended and I was so thankful that there was a strong representation of our own Aboriginal community. It was one of those rare times when I didn't feel like speaking but literally had to force myself to share the story one more time. I told myself, You have to do this for Beatrice. I didn't want people saying 'sorry' to me. They should be saying 'sorry' to my mum – she had the worst pain and the worst life out of all of us.

I was never told exactly what the Welfare wrote in that letter to my mother except that she should have all her children dressed and when and where she should put them on the train. Word spread quickly and all of the family, including grandparents, brothers and sisters, gathered together to try to console her. They all cried with broken hearts. They had heard of this happening to many families who had come off missions and now the government had struck fear in our happy little camp. They discussed hiding from the Welfare and the police, but they knew if she didn't obey the letter that the police would come and place the children in a utility and take them to the city. I only know that *that train* was full of Aboriginal children.

After the service, we, the Aboriginal community, stood in the grounds of the cathedral. So many people kissed my tears, hugged me and expressed their deep sentiment. I can honestly say that I have met people who were so very sincere and who were not ashamed to say 'sorry'.

I was glad it was night. It had been a long day. All day

my thoughts turned towards my first home, the camp and its people. What were they feeling today? Looking back, I can see what an important event Sorry Day was, but on that particular day I was the little girl on the train again, and the journey was just as long as it had been in 1960.

In March 1998, I attended a school reunion. My friend Deanne from high school, who had also been my brides-maid, organised the evening. The reunion was mainly for our own small group of girls who used to sit beneath the old Moreton Bay fig tree. It was wonderful to see what lovely women we had all grown into and I was interested to hear about their families and careers. As I looked across the room I saw a familiar figure – Rhonda, the Aboriginal girl whom I'd avoided in high school. Although Rhonda was not part of our immediate group, I was delighted she wanted to attend.

After the meal we all shared aspects of our life but I chose not to share as I wanted to listen to the others' stories. Two hours had passed and I was unaware that Rhonda had been observing me. Then she came and sat next to me and as we hugged she said, 'You're the only reason I came tonight, to see how you've turned out.' I felt humbled. I apologised for not befriending her at school but back then I was so angry with my people for sending me away, plus I was in denial. She then confessed that as a teenager she also was in denial. She told me, 'People would treat you like dirt and I hated that.'

Rhonda wanted to know if I had met my family and how I tracked them down. I listened with empathy as she revealed that she had been removed from her family and fostered out. She had only started to make enquiries four years ago and was starting to get to know her mob. I told her I had been on my healing journey for fifteen years and it takes a long time to get the answers to the burning questions of the heart. A new friendship began that night and I am so glad that one more of the sunburnt children has come home and whose spirit is begining to heal.

The next month I had the unique experience of reading my chapter, 'Joy Ride', at the Sydney Writers' Festival. I was nervous about reading in front of my two aunts and brother. Aunty Ivy came from Walgett, while Aunty Tam, Widdy and his partner Rita travelled from Coonamble. I was thrilled that they could be with me and loved the expressions on the aunts' faces as they were overwhelmed with the luxury of one of the most expensive hotels in Sydney. They rolled around on the bed laughing, saying, 'Fancy two black gins from the bush bein in this place.'

On the night, Widdy and Rita stood on the steps of the Sydney Town Hall toasting a glass of wine to the passing traffic and joking, saying, 'If only the folks back home could see us now.' Rita couldn't get over how the wine was free, saying, 'Robby would have come if he knew there was free drinks.' It was such a happy time to be together and for me to see them enjoying the moment. Inside, the room was filled with national and international authors, publishers, and media personnel. I was totally unaware of this, only wondering how my family would react to the painful story about the train – and yet having them in attendance was powerful as they knew the story I was reading was only too true.

Whenever I see a train, or cross railway tracks, instantly I recall the train ride. Likewise, when I see a woman with a red hat she reminds me of the Welfare lady. After the second reading at the writers' festival, one of the many people who wanted to speak to me was a woman who wore a red hat. She gently held my hand, looked at me with compassion, and softly said, 'I am a white woman in a red hat. I am not the lady in your story but I want you to know we are not all like her. I want to say how very sorry I am for what happened. Please keep telling your story as we need to hear it.'

She was right, I did have a negative attitude to white women who wore red hats. I said, 'Thank you for doing that for me as now when I see a woman with a red hat I will think of you.' I felt free from the chains of assumption. When I was freed I knew then the healing strength of love.

Every Minute of
the Future

By September 1998 the contract with Random House for my book had been completed and an editor assigned to my book, Debra Adelaide, from Sydney. According to the terms of the contract Debra would make necessary corrections, then after I checked any changes the manuscript would be forwarded for typesetting. I was excited at the prospect, and to think the book was now one step closer, but never imagined what the next six months held for me.

Debra requested I send the disk of the manuscript but this was not as easy as it sounds: I had only taught myself to use a computer in the previous two years and the hard disk had multiple copies of various chapters. It took me months to go through them all to find the final version. I got so frustrated that I wouldn't turn the computer on for weeks at a time. When I was in the mood I could spend three hours searching and then correct perhaps one chapter before going to bed.

Five years had passed since Ron injured his back and as it never improved he was consequently unable to re-enter the workforce. The first year was the hardest for me as I was in denial and could not accept that our lives would be altered permanently. In the second year Ron was so frustrated with my attitude that our relationship was severely strained. He left home and we were separated for six long weeks, but it gave us both breathing space and time to define what we both wanted and needed. I did not realise that Ron had lost so much self-confidence due to not being the breadwinner, and how much he hated to be at home while I worked. I had told him it was my turn now, and was thankful that I had university qualifications, otherwise we would have been on welfare.

Ron only sat to watch the news on television, otherwise he kept busy throughout the day. He taught himself electronics and started fixing all our electrical appliances, stereos, CD players, and even three photocopiers he had in the shed that needed repairing. As well as these interests Ron was still involved with his volunteer organisation, CREST. He was voted in as Operations Director and this filled in the long hours of the day and provided a challenge and gave him more contact with people.

These interests kept him busy but our relationship deteriorated again and subsequently we separated once more, only this time it lasted for almost four months. We were living together but not hearing each other. We had our own point of view and we both had to learn to listen, to hear, understand and compromise. Finally at one point, he knelt beside me and said, 'I don't want this to end.' That was when we both fell in love with each other again. What had happened? We got so busy and forgot to take care of our first priority, each other. People do change over the years and although you don't like it, you must accept it. When communication starts to break down you can be sure you're heading into rough seas. When the communication stops so does the affection, then comes anger followed by stubbornness. I had grieved for three years, for all the changes, for the fact that we would never holiday again, but mostly because I had lost the dream of living happily ever after. I had a fear of growing old together.

In the fourth year, Ron took up a new hobby of breeding birds. He built one aviary, and within twelve months he had twenty budgies, six quails and twelve cockatiels. He had one cockatiel which lived in the house and which talked, whistled, head banged to country music and drank Coke from Ron's glass. Ron then hand-raised a green budgie which hated Mark and myself but loved Ron. This green-feathered excuse for a bird was a woman hater in my hands but in Ron's he was a sook, so that's what Ron called him, 'Sookie'. This bird talked day and night. I am sure he was hyperactive. Sookie imitated the voices of four people and brought so much laughter into our house. Adding to his collection early one Sunday morning was an escaped pied cockatiel that flew onto Ron's shoulder, and naturally this bird was called 'Sunday'. Ron loved this new hobby. He became a registered bird breeder, and was happy again. By the following year his aviaries multiplied to three which divided into breeding sections totalling ten compartments. He was so tender-hearted and gentle with each baby bird that hatched. One morning he found a one-day-old quail drowning in the water container. If Ron had been a minute later it would have been too late, but he picked up the chick and kept it warm in the palm of his hand blowing warm air from his breath on it for fifteen minutes, then placing it in a home-made incubator. The chick survived, and I will always remember it, the size of a peanut, lying helpless in the hand of a gentle giant.

By September 1998 Ron had one hundred and thirty native parrots chirping in our backyard. Spring always brought baby quarrions, rosellas, budgies and quails, but this year's spring didn't warm our hearts. Ron had not been well. The doctor thought he may have an infectious disease from the birds. Most days were taken up by visiting doctors, having x-rays and spending a lot of time waiting. He was referred from one doctor to another.

The night before we were to go to the hospital specialist and learn the results of x-rays, I was sitting in the lounge room praying. Ron had gone to bed early as he was in pain and tired from another day of worrying and sitting around for hours waiting to see doctors. As I sat alone thinking about Ron, his pain, the x-rays, and anxious about what we may be told the next day, the Lord promised me, 'I will not take you anywhere that I have not been before you.' I was in awe but didn't take full hold of it. I wanted to believe it but didn't have enough faith. It gave me hope but I was still uncertain about what was going to happen next.

As we drove to the hospital I quietly reminded myself of the words I had been given the night before. Although we were early Ron still had an hour's wait and while by now we both thought that some lumps on his face and neck may be cancerous, we were not prepared for the news that Ron had lung cancer and that it was well established in the left lung. We took it calmly, mostly because of shock. This doctor referred Ron to another doctor in a specialist hospital for confirmation.

The next morning while Ron went outside to warm the car up, I went back inside the house, nervously opened up my Bible and claimed another verse that said, 'Trust in the Lord, be not afraid for I am with thee,' and so for the rest of that week I claimed a verse for every day. I prayed for ten good years.

A fortnight later we were informed the cancer was more advanced than originally thought, plus it was inoperable and incurable. No doctor would tell us how much time he had other than to say some clients go six months, some may have one year, while some people go five years. As we drove home I told Ron, 'We'll just take one day at a time.' I prayed that the Lord would give us five good years.

When we got home Ron went into the shed and started working. The phone was ringing hot and Ron took call after call while I sat in the backyard crying. How could I manage all this on my own? He would sit for hours in front of the aviaries listening to the different calls of the parrots and watching their antics. He knew every bird and which were breeding pairs. It was a rewarding hobby but now I panicked as I didn't know the first thing about the birds. It took hours to feed and water them and clean out the cages. I wept, as just the thought of cleaning out the shed was a nightmare. Ron had more stuff in the shed than I had in the house. How would I fix things? Our household operated along the traditional roles, me in the house and Ron in the shed. Ron was the fix-it man. How could I learn how to repair everything?

The shock of the news and the fear of the future dulled

my senses and I could not predict what information I would need to know to run a household, but just entertaining the thought for a few short seconds frightened me, so it was easier to concentrate on the present. I couldn't imagine what was in store. Then I got angry: all those cigarettes, all those years, all that money, but now, all this pain.

Ron was in shock for a few days. At the time I thought he had accepted the news so well, as he joked with his mates and was full of hope and refused to let it get to him. I think I was almost relieved when he came to me in the bathroom two days later and held me so tightly and wept his heart out. He held me and kissed me and I felt secure and safe. He told me he loved me and that he was sorry. He didn't want to hurt me. He said, 'I can get through this if you're there with me.' He assured me how he was going to prove to the doctors that this wasn't going to beat him. He then said, 'We have to get a lot of things done.' He rattled off all the things that needed fixing, then cleaning up the shed and going to the solicitor.

Ron had just had his first panic attack and realised how much he wanted to achieve, and so he began repairs. I will never forget the expression on his face. The strain of trying to withhold tears filled with sorrow and love. He spent the best part of that day sorting out tools, equipment, electronic boards and other things kept in storage.

I think Ron had poor sleep that night as he was making a list of what he needed to do. The next morning he got out of bed at six o'clock, having decided to grab an early start on the day. After feeding the birds, his next task was to fix the seal on the fridge and as he bent to undo the screws his back twisted, and he was unable to move for two hours. After visiting our family doctor at eleven o'clock, then after spinal x-rays, bone scans, and the worst pain imaginable, Ron was admitted into hospital at three o'clock. He was unable to walk. He complained about the indescribable pain in his back and shoulders. He told his mates the back pain was killing him. He never had any pain in the lungs, not even a cough, and so we believed it was the old original back injury.

I was nervous. I am not a nervous person, I can cope with a lot, but this made me anxious. I came home from the hospital and around midnight I decided to look at the x-rays and read the doctor's report. Sheer horror slapped me in the face as I realised how seriously ill Ron was. The cancer had already spread to his bones. I knew we were dealing with a wildfire. I think I cried almost all night. I raced up to the hospital early the next morning with an urgency to speak with Ron about the diagnosis. It was time for truth and we didn't have an hour to waste. With his arms wrapped around me, we made specific plans for the future including the will and the burial. After it had been discussed, I knew his wishes and there was no need to bring it up again. We then set about dealing with the day-to-day issues of surviving, healing and repairing. I prayed for one good year.

Ron made a miraculous recovery and he came home four days later. The next week he had to register with the oncology unit. From our first visit to the Mater Hospital oncology unit, all the staff were just magnificent, devoted and caring. On our first visit Ron was very nervous, not knowing what to expect. We arrived at eight-thirty in the morning and in the first room we entered we saw ten people waiting. We overheard that these people were waiting for blood tests. The second waiting room had twenty people waiting to see the doctor. I hadn't expected so many people at this time of day. I whispered to Ron, 'Look, we're not alone.'

The doctor had arranged a meeting for chemotherapy education. We met with a nurse who informed us of our options, and the pharmacist who clarified the side effects of individual drugs. We were given three days to make up our minds what treatment we preferred. It was a decison only Ron could and should make. He decided to go with chemotherapy. The staff took all the fear out of it for us. Ron had a good, strong attitude. He was determined to beat the cancer. He commenced chemotherapy in October which was to last for six months. He breezed through it with the help of painkillers. His back injury on top of the chemo treatment made him very tired and we started going to bed by ten o'clock. We both had always been night owls but the uncertainty of the future and the stress made our bodies very tired.

We were tired from shock, denial, fears, coping and encouraging each other and our sons. I recall there was an election and as we left the voting booth I wondered whether this would be the last time Ron would vote, or would he see our beautiful jacaranda trees bloom again? Would this be his last birthday? Although these were the fears within my own heart, I never mentioned them to Ron. I think we both wanted to be strong for each other. In November Ron's pain doubled and so did the painkillers. His back pain became unbearable so he was put on a course of morphine whilst at the same time undergoing chemotherapy every week. At times Ron was so weak that I wondered if he would make Christmas. I prayed for six good months.

We gained strength by the courage we saw in other cancer patients. Cancer has no respect for age, sex, race, religion or status. I kept praying and Ron kept a very positive attitude with every hope of beating this thing. One week before Christmas, his body was racked with pain but he refused to see the doctors as he believed it was the chemo tiring him. I didn't want to think about Christmas this year, there was nothing merry going on inside our house. As I stood at the deli a stranger, a gentleman, smiled and said, 'Merry Christmas to you and your family' and I burst into tears. Up until that Christmas I always had expectations of gifts but this year I had a coldness within and I wished we could ignore the season.

But I came home from work one day to find our Christmas tree, decorations and lights standing brightly in the lounge room. Mark, Tim and Sherriden, Tim's partner, had organised it. Life didn't seem real, and there was no such thing as a normal day any more, but that afternoon I realised I had to try to make things seem as normal as possible for Ron and our kids. I was so ashamed for past conversations about gifts and it seemed to me that I had to learn that Ron was my present. Christmas Day felt pretentious. I didn't want to think if this was his last or I would have cried all day; instead I focused on how I could make it into a bright, good day. He was the best present I could ever have. How sad though that it took me a lifetime to realise it. Hugs for over twenty-five years were taken for granted as for the past week Ron was too weak to do this and all we could do was touch his index finger to say goodnight. I couldn't stroke his arm or hair as everything felt like electric shocks and I felt disconnected, distant and even rejected.

Irene, Ron's youngest sister, had planned a big party on

Boxing Day. She had driven down from Kingaroy and catered for the whole thing herself. It was an opportunity for Ron to see forty relations turn up, but he spent most of the time keeping warm in bed. He was so very, very sick, that it only made everyone so sad to see him in such dreadful pain.

The next morning we went to casualty and after a three-hour observation he was sent home. The morphine intake was increased by five times the dose. Ron then sat out two unbearable nights. He had not slept in forty-eight hours and was nearly insane with pain. In the morning I phoned for an ambulance and Ron was admitted into hospital for the second time. The morphine hadn't helped.

When the doctor said he would refer us to the Palliative Care Team I knew we were in dire straits. Three days later Ron was taken off the morphine as he was found to be morphine resistant, and instead he was given a combination of several other drugs. I was sleeping at home but I wanted to stay with Ron as I knew it wouldn't be easy, but I was not prepared for what I saw and heard. For the next three days and nights I watched my husband hallucinating and coming down from the morphine. It was very sad, disturbing and exhausting. I never want to see anybody go through such torment ever again in my life. Ron had not had sleep for five nights.

The nursing staff in ward 5A were like angels in navy uniforms. I slept at the hospital for four weeks. I am not the hero here, Ron was. I kept telling our sons and visitors, 'We have the easy part, Ron has the hard part.' He was so courageous. In the first week of being admitted Ron lost the use of his legs. All of his dreams were about running and walking. Ron could never walk slow. It was always a brisk walk. It was a habit from work. He would jump down four feet from the lathe and walk quickly to the front of the machine and change a tool or check the cut and then climb back up on top of the lathe, and then do the same thing again fifteen minutes later. I spent hour after hour massaging his feet, moving them so he was comfortable. We both thought it was temporary but we became concerned when the numbness crept into his fingers and hands. He kept looking at his hands and rubbing them. He exclaimed, 'They're all I've got left. I need them.' This has to be temporary, I told myself.

My heart grieved at his words as I too looked at his hands and remembered how skilled he was with them. Able to repair anything. Build anything out of steel. Rebuild cars that were written off. Turn up parts on the lathe for anything from washing machines to wheelchairs. I remembered how he drew up plans for, then made, a whizz-bang steel go-cart for the boys when Darren was eight and Tim was four years old. It was the envy of the boys in the neighbourhood. Once it was stolen and when I approached the father of the boy who stole it, he simply said, 'Okay, if your husband made it, take it.' I reflected on the gentle hands that wrapped around me every night, cradled his baby boys, held microphones and built bird aviaries, and that now had no feeling and could not grasp a spoon. Many times I had seen movies with people feeding their loved ones who were paralysed and I thought it would be a horrible thing to have to do, but now it was my turn. God gave me the grace and it was so easy. I was glad I could do something for my husband. It was a privilege and I allowed Ron's parents and sister to have that privilege also.

I had no time to grieve as there was too much work to be done. Ron never complained once in hospital. Ron never swore either. I could hear other male patients swearing their heads off. The nurses said, 'It's the drugs and they don't know they are doing it,' but Ron didn't. I washed him several times a day as the sweat would pour out of him. One day he went through eight T-shirts. I had to give him his tablets and feed him. Wash him, roll him, turn him over from side to side so he was comfortable. Rub him with oil and just be there beside him.

A week after Ron had been in hospital he had a MRI scan done and we were hit with worse news. He had a four-inch tumour in his back which was pressing on the spinal cord in one place. He underwent six radiation treatments, but it was too late. The radiation was unable to shrink the tumour.

One doctor drew the curtains around me and, as sensitively and caringly as he could, warned me that the next forty-eight hours were critical. If Ron made it through, then he would watch to see if he made it through the weekend, and if he made it through the weekend then we were to just take one day at a time. We were on borrowed time. I prayed for one day at a time.

We had been blessed with time to put our house in order. Ron finalised a will and other business. Next he asked me to call the boys in for a meeting and to cancel all other visitors that night. Bravely he told them the truth, what he wanted for their future. He told the boys what terrific partners they had, meaning Lindy and Sherriden. He told Darren and Lindy how glad he was to have seen his beautiful grandchildren for fourteen months. He smiled as he recalled, 'It was a shock at first, but that doesn't matter now.'

It wasn't a shock. I was shattered. I had been in Sydney for a four-day conference and Ron had phoned. He was cautious, hesitant, and I said, 'Just say it.' He slowly said, 'You're going to be a grandmother.' I was delighted, and after I found out which son I asked, 'When?' After a pause came the reply: 'By the time you drive back to Newcastle.' Twelve hours later Darren phoned to tell us that Lindy had had a boy and a girl. Ten weeks premature. I cried for a week. Lindy and her parents were beautiful people and they all wanted to tell us but it was up to Darren. When I asked him why he didn't tell us he said, 'I couldn't, I just couldn't.' I agonised over that for quite a few weeks. Was it because he was the good son or because of the values, beliefs and expectations I had, and would hope that my children would hold to also? Was it because I was Aboriginal and he was ashamed of me, or because he didn't want to share his life with us? I had to pull myself together immediately and show him that I loved him and loved the babies. I had to show him that a family pulls together in the good times and the bad, but more than that, we had two tiny grandchildren fighting for their lives and I covered them with prayer. And Ron and I were very proud grandparents. I was overcome with joy when I learned the babies were given Aboriginal names – Beau Lane Michael (Lane means 'good') and Kiyarna Louise (Kiyarna means 'water bird on the throne').

Right now Ron was ever so thankful that he saw them and he thought they were fantastic. He apologised for lost opportunities and then he told me what he wanted me to do in the future. He told me that I was his future. It took a big man to say all the things he did. We all expressed our own personal regrets. We all cried together. Time was running out and we were all in a state of shock. There were so many things to say but there were so many tears to cry first.

So many relationships were healed that week. Ron had always jumped to help people and now he was having the biggest impact on so many lives. It was a time for family and friends to redefine themselves. The soul-searching made people prioritise and realise what really was important in life. This experience made our boys grow up overnight, their maturity was evident. How hard it must have been for each of them to see their father's deterioration.

Ron's bladder ceased working and his bowel became blocked. Our plan was to take Ron home when he opened his bowel. There was very little circulation in his body so I put work socks on his feet and special thermal stockings on his arms. One night I only had thirty minutes' sleep, another night I was up every twenty minutes, but usually I was up every hour or couple of hours keeping him dry, massaging his legs and fluffing pillows.

Every second day Ron was placed in a spa for a bath. As he was paralysed, the wardsmen would place him on a specially designed trolley which could be lowered into a spa with hot water spouting from its jets. Ron loved this. For ten minutes he could float and be completely pain-free. One time I left Ron and his father, Jack, together. As I waited outside the bathroom, I knew it would be hard for Jack to bath his son as it would bring back memories of Ron being a little boy, but I knew they needed time together. When I returned Jack squeezed my hand and whispered, 'Thanks, sweetheart.' Unfortunately, drying, powdering, dressing and returning Ron to bed left him exhausted as all the prodding, lifting, turning and rolling took all his energy and he would sleep and just wake for meals for the remainder of the day.

As I sat silently beside him I would remember all my husband's habits, likes and dislikes in life. He was such a clean man, he would always have a shower and wear freshly ironed clothes whenever he went shopping or just to pay bills. When buying clothes he always trusted my choice of selection. I didn't want people to think I was a controlling wife so I would say, 'You pick out some clothes you like this time,' but his reply was always the same: 'I don't have any taste, you know what looks good.'

During those endless hours watching and waiting, I remembered how we once fought for over two hours because I had bought him a grey pigskin jacket. It was half price. I knew he would look distinguished in it. I thought I would spend that amount on clothes for myself in six months. He was worth it and it would last for years, plus he needed something warm. Ron was angry because I had used the rent money. We just did not have spare money or other accounts that we could pinch from Peter to pay Paul. I cried and cried as he yelled at me. All I could base my argument on was the fact that I wanted to give him a gift, a beautiful gift, at half price, because he was worth something nice. But somehow over the next few weeks we caught up with the rent, and Ron indeed wore the jacket with pride. If we went to socials at least one person would admire the jacket and make a comment like, 'Classy jacket,' or 'You've got expensive taste.' Ron would proudly say, 'My wife bought it for me,' and we would look at each other and exchange a cheeky smile.

I wanted to make people happy. I loved buying gifts, it was love in action, but my gift giving frustrated Ron. Arguments meant he would lecture and I would listen. It always

came back to 'the budget'. I couldn't articulate my view-
point but he did it so well. As I looked at his handsome
face in that bed my heart was so sad, yet in the midst of
that pain was a joy that I had showered him with gifts and
I didn't regret one dollar.

All Ron could see from the bed was the sky and clouds drifting by. The room was so small and the air conditioning was
not working properly. Finally I had to make the decision to
move him into the hospice where the staff could give him
more personal care. The room was bigger, cooler, plus Ron
could hear the waterfall in the courtyard, see the shrubs and
hear the birds chirping and watch them gaily hopping
around. The hours of the days dragged on. Ron hadn't eaten
for over nine days and his bowels were still blocked. Lyn
Hughes, my friend from church, phoned me one day to give
encouragement. Lyn was praying for me over the phone and
these words rang in my ears and carried me through that
week: 'Lord, we just pray for every minute of the future, for
you know what the future will bring.'

I knew I had made the right decision to move Ron to
the hospice the next afternoon when there was a short sun
shower and Ron commented on the smell of rain on the
concrete. He kept his head turned toward the glass sliding
doors watching the gentle rain fall. He said to his father,
'I'd love to be able to run out in it, Pop.' I pretended I was
arranging flowers in a vase but managed to catch a glimpse
of Jack's misty eyes as he reacted to his son's words.

Tim and Sherriden had walked into his room the day
before with a huge bouquet of native flowers that cost $50.
Ron was so tired that he weakly asked, 'Who are they for?'
Sherriden replied, 'They're for you, Dad.' Ron replied,

'Oh, you shouldn't do that, daughter.' She later told me it was worth it because he called her daughter. Ron's mother, Betty, spent a lot of time with Ron too, but usually when she was with him I would go and have coffee or a short break. All January our friends and family were a wonderful support through this stressful, tragic time. Some of my brothers and sisters travelled all the way from Coonamble and Canberra to see Ron, the boys and me. Neil couldn't drive into the city but I kept in regular contact by phone with Mum and Neil. Mum was upholding us all in prayer.

The day before Ron's last day the professor came to his bed and asked him, 'What do you want me to do for you?' Ron could have asked for a miracle, for healing, or any number of things, but he humbly said, 'I just wish I could stand up and have a pee.' He was so unselfish. I thought of all the things we take for granted. Life, legs and love.

I had no idea there were only twenty-four hours left. I think I believed we still had a few months. I remember starting to feel relief when his bowels finally opened and I thought we would be going home the next day. All night long, I kept buzzing nurses. We would change the linen, wash Ron, make him comfortable, turn the light out and just start to drift off, and then he would want a nurse again. I only got twenty minutes' sleep after six o'clock in the morning. It was a long night.

Ron had two hours' sleep and when he woke he was hungry and wanted some breakfast but two mouthfuls were all he could eat. I phoned Ron's parents to come earlier than usual as I needed to get a couple of hours' sleep. They arrived around nine o'clock. I had some sleep between ten and eleven o'clock. I woke to hear Jack, Betty and Father

Tony Stace talking about trout fishing trips on the Barrington Tops. I knew Ron could hear the conversation and I thought he would be picturing every stream and causeway. He hadn't been up his mountain for over five years since he injured his back. Every day Ron would play his favourite country song, 'My Heart is Still in the Bush', and I knew it really was.

After midday Ron's breathing became so laboured that Jack suggested I call the boys in. They had been notified and were finding ways of transport. Tim and Sherriden and Mark came within the hour. Darren was at work and had to organise relief. Ron's sister, Roslyn, had gone home to Tamworth for two days to arrange school uniforms for her two teenagers and was already on the XPT returning to Newcastle. Irene and her family were in Kingaroy. Ron's youngest brother, Ray, was working at Willow Tree in the Upper Hunter Valley.

I had phoned Mum to tell her I had called for the boys but I said there was no need for her to come, the best thing she could do was to pray, so I was so suprised to see her walk through the door at three o'clock. Neil was too sick to drive her in and so Mum had asked a neighbour to bring her. Ron was unable to talk, but held tight onto her hand as she spoke to him. She kept saying, 'I had this feeling that I had to come, so strange. I tried to ignore it but I was being urged.' I knew that he had called her. Ron lovingly smiled at her and kept nodding his head as if to say, 'Yes, thank you for coming.' Mum and Betty stood around the bed, both holding Ron's hands. We had been blessed to have both in-laws love each other. As I took a five-minute coffee break I thought it would probably happen in the middle of the night when I was all alone.

Roslyn arrived at the hospice at four o'clock and Darren and Lindy were there thirty minutes later. Our youngest son Mark had been at the hospice since lunchtime. He sat quietly in shock in the corner. Each one of us tried to coax him into going to the bed and holding Ron's hand. I told him, 'Daddy's waiting for you,' but Mark just sat on the fold-up bed, glued, frozen, crying. A few weeks prior Mark had made a tape of all of Ron's favourite country music. That afternoon, Mark just played it over and over on the little cassette player. Mark finally took his grandma home and came straight back to the hospice.

Hour after hour passed by. It took every bit of effort for Ron to breathe. He wasn't wheezing, just labouring. Every single heart in that room ached. It was so painful to watch Ron holding on. Someone mentioned that there was a gift for me from Ron for Valentine's Day but I said, 'I'll wait till then, I'll need it then.' As I sat beside Ron I started to whisper to him, telling him, 'It's time to go fishing. Just think of a beautiful stream on the Barrington and go there.' I reasurred him that he had done everything he could. That we would be all right, to think of himself now. 'You gave it a good fight,' I told him, 'it's okay to let go.' His eyes were closed and he tried three times to say, 'I love you.' I looked at the clock: it was five-thirty. I silently began praying. I thought Ron wouldn't want to be here for years paralysed in bed. I wanted Ron to have his dignity. I realised then that there was no colour in death. Whether we are black or white all we could ever want is to die with peace and dignity, surrounded by the people who love us.

At five-fifty Roslyn became agitated and nervous, and kept saying, 'Shouldn't we do something?' Twice she said it and then she asked, 'Do you want to hold hands and pray?' We all gathered around the bed, even Mark joined us, and I prayed giving thanks for Ron and his life. The young girls began crying, it was so hard not to fall apart too. After I prayed I put on a gospel tape thinking it would be soft and comforting. It was during the chorus of the first song called 'Sheltered in the Arms of God' that Ron took his last breath and fell asleep. The chorus said 'I'll fall asleep and wake, sheltered in the arms of God.'

I was stunned. I just stood there. I couldn't cry, I was so relieved he was out of pain. Darren held Ron's other hand and said, 'Dad's not in pain any more,' and I replied, 'No, sweetheart, he's not in any more pain.'

He then said, 'You're so brave, Mum.'

I said, 'Darren, this isn't me, you know I'm a real sook, this is answered prayer. God is real. He has given me the strength for every day. Dad gave his heart to the Lord ten days ago and now he is heaven.'

Immediately I was aware of the hollow silence not only in the room but also outside. There were no sounds coming from the corridor. No phones, buzzers, voices, footsteps or the clanging of food trays. It was as if we were all frozen in time. I stood beside the bed holding Ron's hand trying to accept what I had just witnessed. I let the gospel tape play on right to the end and then turned it over so side two could run through.

About ten minutes later I thought, I have to comfort the boys, and I held each one. Just as I held Tim he started to cry. He had been Ron's mate. I had left messages during the past few hours for Ron's doctor to contact us but Dr Martin was unable to get away in time. Now, upon entering the room, she realised what had happened and gave me a sympathetic hug. She then gracefully stepped forward and lovingly took Ron's hand and said, 'Well, Ron, I have only known you for a short time but it has been a privilege and an honour. Thank you for allowing me to come into your life at this very special time in your life.'

The phone beside the bed rarely worked as there weren't enough lines to compensate for the demand, but oddly enough when I tried I was able to dial straight out. I knew Mum would take the news badly as she was still praying for a miracle even that very afternoon. Just three hours ago, Ron's mother held his left hand and his mother-in-law held his right hand while they talked to each other. Hoping to coax her into a response as she held Ron's hand I said, 'Mum, Ron's been a wonderful son-in-law hasn't he?'

Her eyes flashed with disagreement as she said, 'What do you mean was, he is still here. I will not give up, no, no. Of course Ron was a good son-in-law, the best. I always loved Ron from the first time I met him and I think he loved me too.'

I wanted Ron's parents and his sister to spend as much time as possible with him so I stepped into the courtyard to sit with my children and their partners. Mark and Tim were in their own world of thoughts. Darren and Lindy had gone to a shopping centre to collect cardboard boxes so we could pack everything in the room and go home. Sherriden had a puzzled expression as her gaze moved from the water-fall up to the blue sky and back to the waterfall. There it was again – this amazing utter silence. Not one bird call. Not one vehicle passed. There was no sound whatsoever. I thought it was my ears but Tim and Sherro said, 'It's been like this ever since Dad left.'

There had been a thunderstorm at five o'clock but now, just after six, the sun was shining and the clouds had all disappeared. The silence was stunning. I thought of my brothers and sisters in Coonamble and I said, 'All we need is a magpie.' As I spoke the words a magpie flew down and sat on the edge of the waterfall. It was so amazing that it left the three of us speechless. It was a sign they were here with us in spirit. Ron brought us all together.

When I was given the forty-eight-hour alert I had asked each of our sons if Dad took bad in the middle of the night, did they want me to call them in to say goodbye? They all indicated that they preferred not to. I can't blame them. I didn't know what to expect myself. I was scared of the end. I had only seen Hollywood's version of death. I really didn't want to be by myself either. I kept thinking about what we had all witnessed and it was just amazing. It wasn't planned. God's timing was perfect. He was so gracious and full of mercy. Having witnessed with our own eyes took the fear of death away. Ron was always a gentleman – why should he cease to be one even in his last hour on this earth?

After every family member took their turn to say goodbye we packed all of Ron's possessions, gifts and flowers: it was time to leave. The boys wanted to take me home. As we walked toward the car I wanted to run back to be with Ron and I felt I was deserting him. It was daylight saving and the sun just setting as we walked across the car park at eight-fifteen. Overlooking the city was the most brilliant orange sunset. The clouds had a golden ridge like a halo and the windows in houses and cars reflected the golden beams that covered the city. Even out in the car park the eerie blanket of silence confounded us. The boys were commenting about it again and I tried to reason it that we were all in shock, but my dear friend Bev had come to the hospice and witnessed it all too. She said, 'This is a very busy street, the traffic doesn't stop flowing here even at this time of day and I can't believe there is not one car in sight, either way. It's as if Ron was giving us a sign to let us know he is at peace.'

Back in the house that all our children had grown up in, we recalled different events in their life, some of the funny things Dad had done or said. Darren and Lindy stayed until ten o'clock and left but Tim, Sherriden and Mark sat around talking about the last few weeks. At one in the morning I crawled into bed and then the three of them came and sat on the bed and continued to talk about Dad. I still hadn't cried. I was just glad he was out of pain. As the clock chimed two I said, 'I had better get some sleep, I didn't get any last night and I'm tired.'

I sat in bed numbed by the day's events and then I had my first panic attack, the fear of reality, of being a widow, alone, unable to cope and fix things. My heart and soul felt flooded with fear. I thought: 'How am I going to do this? How can I pay the bills? How can I keep the birds? How can I keep the house running?' Just then in the darkness I sensed Ron's presence standing beside the bed. I thought, 'No, I am imagining this.' Then I felt him hold my two hands, firmly yet gently, and heard him saying, 'Don, Don.' All my fear left and I had joy. I had hope. He was still around. Then I fell asleep and didn't wake until seven and it was the first day in a new era.

Ron's mates came to feed the birds. My sister and her family came from Coonamble to be with me. Although we requested no flowers I was overwhelmed with the thirteen bouquets that were delivered to our house. We received one hundred and ten sympathy cards. At the funeral, donations raised $350 for Ward 5A to buy something for the spa to help other paraplegics. Over five hundred people attended Ron's funeral. Although the boys and I didn't want a didge player, on the day young Les Saxby turned up and played for Ron. I stroked Mark's hand as if to say, 'It's all right, Les wanted to do it for Dad.' I think it was the first time a didgeridoo was ever played in the old Baptist church that was steeped in tradition.

The sound that permeated through the building brought tears to many eyes as it was a spiritual experience for them. Ron had the finest tributes from friends and the organisations he was affiliated with. Even the boys who were in his EK Holden that day twenty-six years ago when Ron first saw me and had told them, 'I'm going to marry her one day,' all came, only now we were all in our forties.

It was the first time at the church that a country song on tape was played at a funeral. I arranged for Ron's favourite song by Brian Letton, 'My Heart is Still in the Bush', to be played. Brian had phoned Ron from a recording studio in Tamworth when he learned Ron was so ill. I don't know what Brian was saying to Ron, but he cried all the time. Ron was so humbled to think Brian took the time to do that for him.

We decided on an all-white floral arrangement for the coffin. Tim insisted that Dad would want common old bracken fern, so the enormous bouquet sat on a layer of bracken fern. Unbeknown to us, until she phoned to ask if it would be all right, Aunty Del had picked some bracken fern from Hunter Springs as she left the property to come down the mountain for the funeral, to place on the coffin. I told her that Ron would love it. Aunty Lorna recited Ron's favourite poem called 'Tubrabucca'.

As I had spoken so many times for Newcastle I wanted to speak for Ron at the funeral. We knew better and worse, richer and poorer, in sickness and health. We were three months short of being married for twenty-six years. We proved that reconciliation could work. There was one wreath leaning against the wall at the back of the church and later when I read the card I found it was from Carmel Bird in Melbourne. She'd written the words, 'Love doesn't have a colour.' She didn't know I'd said those very words in my tribute.

I would like to thank my Heavenly Father for the grace, strength and peace that helped me through the hardest hours in my life. Ron gave his heart to the Lord ten days before he was called home. I know I will see him again. Ron told his mates that he'd had a wonderful life, that if he had his time over, he would do it all the same, he wouldn't change anything, he'd had a fantastic time. He was a man from the bush, he was a man of humanity and a great Novocastrian.

I can't explain everything that I experienced, smelled, felt and dreamed about in the following months but I would like to think they were signs that I was not alone, or not to be afraid. I started to cry three weeks later. I came up with question after question. My body was so tired because grieving is hard work, for mind, body and soul. A thousand words and a thousand memories would trigger the heart and bring me to tears and each time I had to recover and wait for the next southerly wind to hit. This was the winter of my life. I missed my husband so much. I cried myself to sleep for eight months. The grieving process is hard work. Our people call it 'sorry time' and it does take a long, long time. I was sorry about a lot of things. In between the tears, the visible and invisible memories flowed like continuous lace, so fragile, delicate, linking love and life to time and sequence. Every episode of *This is Your Life* made me weep and I thought about Ron's life and contribution to society and deep within I heard a voice say, 'It is up to you to bring recognition of his life.' So it should be. He said that I was his future. It is all the adjusting and accepting realisations like being a widow, a single parent, not having a partner to problem solve, and not feeling safe. And other things like repairing the cars for registration. Having a man in the house, I felt safe but now I was insecure. I prayed that God would protect Mark and me through the night watch. There was also all the administration details and legal affairs to attend to as well as supporting our boys through their grief and loss.

I am learning to follow the footprints of our matriarchs. I am not going through anything new, they have walked before me. They survived and I will too. Our spirits are so strong, we soar through the emotional earthquakes. Those crises that turn our world upside down. We have to for our children, for the next generation. We have a sacred trust that has been imparted to us by our forefathers and mothers and they are depending on us to be the message stick. When it comes to matters of the heart, we are steel.

I have learned to love better, to pray believing, to be a stronger women, to trust God always, to look forward to heaven and not to take life and love for granted. I am so thankful Ron gave me three adorable, loving sons so I am not alone, and now the eldest son of the eldest son of the eldest son has three sons to carry on his name and spirit.

I have met some of the best and the worst people from both cultures. Some people are like sunshine and you feel warmed by just being around them. The people I like to be with most are the peacemakers. We know each other when we meet because we believe in each other's values. There are a lot of things in life more important than status, money and material possessions. My personal message has always been to promote reconciliation, or as we teach the children, 'walking together'.

I have walked with my brother in writing this book. The promise kept me going. At first I simply wanted to share a story about two special women and honour them both, as I am proud they were both my mothers. The beauty of the story is the cultural experiences that taught me understanding, but the fragrance that wafts between the pages has to be the answered prayers and the gracious acts of providence. Surely this is the sweetest perfume.

God knew me before I was in my mother's womb. He sat beside me in the train. He chose my mothers and my husband. He knew my secret thoughts of suicide and He opened my mouth to speak. He sat with me in the waiting room and comforted me in the valley of the shadow of death until the shadow passed.

I believe that death is not the end because heaven is my destination. The best is yet to come. I don't know about tomorrow but I do know the one who holds tomorrow is interceding for me today and He will be in control of every minute of the future.

I pray that you may know my secret too.

Acknowledgements

With a heart full of gratitude I would like to thank the following:

My heavenly Father for His loving kindness every day of my life and for all the blessings from the people He brought into my life. It is no secret what He can do.

My mum Elizabeth for her prayers, love and encouragement.

My mum Beatrice for loving me enough to 'let me go'.

To all the Welsh and Meehan families for accepting me.

To all the women I have written about, for you have taught me so much.

My sincere thanks to Deb Callaghan, my first publisher, to Jody Lee, and to Debra Adelaide, my editor, who understood me and didn't change the manuscript, which enabled my Aboriginal heart and voice to come through the page.

I would also like to thank Paul Walsh for first publishing 'Joy Ride' and other extracts in *Novocastrian Tales* (Elephant Press, 1997) and to Carmel Bird for including 'Joy Ride' in *The Stolen Children — Their Stories* (Random House, 1998).

And many thanks to all my dear friends who have believed in me and supported me.